An Invitation
To Heal

An Invitation
To Heal

Susan Spalding

cp

Aventine Press

An Invitation to Heal

Copyright © 2004 Susan Spalding

Edited by Kathy O'Dell

Cover art and author photograph by Don McFadden.
www.higherworld.com

The term Directional Healing is a trademark of Susan Spalding.

Published by Aventine Press, LLC
2208 Cabo Bahia
Chula Vista, CA 91914, USA
www.aventinepress.com

Library of Congress Cataloging-in-Publication Data
2004102100
ISBN: 1-59330-142-1
Printed in the United States of America

This book is dedicated to the One Love
that heals and makes all things right.

To the Reader

When I was a young child, I discovered the magic, beauty, and power of books. My life has always been so much bigger, richer, and interesting because of the books that have been meaningful to me. The really good ones inspire me, make me want to be a better person, give me a yardstick for judging my life, free my imagination and my spirit, and trigger profound insights and realizations.

I learned that words and the images they convey are portals, keys to other worlds. Through my studies and experiences with vibrational healing, I have learned that the right words, expressed the right way, can also be keys to healing.

But a key merely represents a potential, a possibility for the opening of a door. It is up to us whether or not to enter therein.

Recently a woman told me that her grown son asked about the energy treatments she was receiving. "What is the purpose of this work? What does it do for you?" he asked. She said that without even thinking, she replied: "It keeps you from suffering so much." I am sure that this is what every sincere writer hopes for—that the work into which he has poured his love and inspiration will to some degree alleviate suffering, heal and uplift those who read it.

And so, dear reader, if any of the keys that are scattered throughout this book fit you at this time, may they enrich your journey and assist you in your quest for health, happiness, and great spiritual adventures!

Susan Spalding

Table of Contents

Part Two
Taking Responsibility – Healing Through Self-Mastery

Part Three
Accepting the Gift – Healing Through Divine Love

Preface

Good health includes having a healthy body, healthy mind, healthy finances, and healthy relationships. This is an invitation to heal your life on all levels through an active, co-working relationship with the Holy Spirit, the creative intelligence of the universe.

Did you know that sacred covenants—God's promise to you and your promise to God—are stored within your heart center? You can learn how to read the sacred agreements written in your heart and find your heart's desire for your life. If you have longed to know your purpose and to feel a deeper connection to life, listen to Spirit's invitation to you.

In addition to your physical anatomy, you have a corresponding energy or spiritual anatomy. A series of energy gates, known as chakras, exist within you. They regulate the flow of energy and information, and provide the pathways through which your body, mind and spirit interact. An energy gate requires the proper vibrational key in order to unlock your body's healing potential.

Perhaps up to this point you have given little thought to the inner mysteries of your body and inner state of being. Maybe you think of the body as a machine that generally works pretty well, and if it gets an ache or pain, you look for the proper mechanic to help repair it, someone in one of the healing arts. But the body is more. It is an extension of your consciousness, and as such it is the wondrous instrument that enables you to experience life in the physical world.

As soul you are a vibrational being not of this world. A body of dense material is needed to cover and protect you. The body also provides the senses that enable you to fully interact with your physical environment. But a lifetime of sensual experience can make you oblivious to the hidden, higher senses, and the secret inner worlds.

All creations in the physical world need upkeep and maintenance. They deteriorate and break down over time. When our bodies begin to suffer, our quality of life goes down. We don't enjoy being in pain or not being active and self-sufficient. It is natural and right to seek ways to enhance our physical well-being. But to seek only physical recovery or cures for our problems is like applying a Band-Aid as a treatment for the most severe illness. The greatest ailment from which we suffer is that we have lost our connection with our true state of being. We no longer hear the voice of soul whispering its desires for this lifetime—to further its spiritual understanding and to advance on its journey home to God. And we suffer, not knowing the cause or cure.

We are powerful beings with stores of untapped resources, but we haven't been told the truth. We have been told that if we eat such and such a diet, take this or that supplement or pill, say this or think that, try this device or technique, we will be healed and life will be wonderful. While some of these things can affect positive changes and even cures, healing runs much deeper and requires more, as we will see in later chapters.

Within us are centers, little known or used, that, when awakened, connect us to every part of God's universe. It is as if we are living in a huge mansion, but we keep ourselves locked in the cellar. It is my wish to share with you a new vision of what healing is, and to provide the opportunity to experience yourself as a vibrational being. Healing is so much more than relieving a symptom or curing a condition. It is the doorway to more spiritual freedom and self-knowledge. Your current state does not have to be your prison, but can be the doorway to your own inner mansions when you have the right key.

So the invitation to heal is an invitation to accept the keys to your own inner mansion. It is really an invitation from yourself to yourself: "Come out of the cellar. Our life is waiting."

Part One

Co-Creating Health–
Becoming a
Co-Worker with God

Chapter 1

When God Calls Your Name

A number of years ago, I joined a new business venture that sounded promising. I went to a training the company offered to learn how to best optimize my chances of success. At one point during the training, we were given a piece of poster paper, some magazine clippings, and told to make a collage of our dreams and goals. We were to take the collage home and then watch our dreams manifest during the coming year. It was great fun placing pictures of a dream house, a nice car, a happy family, vacations, etc., on the paper. When I left the seminar with my collage, however, I still had the same state of consciousness I had brought with me. I still had the same limiting thought patterns and beliefs. I was the same person, just temporarily more motivated and excited. I was still in the cellar, without any clear directions on how to climb out.

A miraculous thing happened to me, however, in 1989, when I had a dream that changed the course of my life. It would be the beginning of many lessons on change. We expect change to happen to us, for something to happen to us that changes our circumstances for the better. However, miracles happen when we realize that change comes through us, from the inside out.

We are actually prepared for the major turning points in our lives many years beforehand. We may not be aware of the importance of the messages in the events around us until later, however, when we look back on our lives. My preparation for such an event began many years before.

When I was a young girl of about ten, my aunt and a friend of hers took me to a drive-in movie one evening. I sat in the back seat of the car mesmerized by the scene unfolding on the screen. A young Scotsman, who had been wondering about his direction and purpose in life, was walking home late one evening through a thick fog. Suddenly, he stopped as he heard a voice call his name.

The mysterious voice in the dark had prevented him from taking a treacherous fall, the dangers of the terrain hidden by the fog. At the moment he heard the voice, he had also been impressed with a sense of his mission. He was to travel to America and become a minister. The movie was *A Man Called Peter* and was based on the biography of Peter Marshall, written by his wife Catherine Marshall.

A man in modern times had heard the voice of God! It had told him what to do. I had not heard of any experiences of personal encounters with the voice of God outside of the Bible stories in Sunday school. How I longed to meet such a person, to hear first hand how one could learn to listen to and follow this inner guidance. How wonderful it would be to have God reveal your own personal mission in life! At that time, I thought only rare and special people could have such a personal encounter with God, and certainly only special people were called. I didn't know then that we are all being called, all of the time.

I didn't know about the nature of soul, that all souls are equal. All are made from the fabric of God's light and sound, infused with love and purpose. In the human consciousness, of course, we are all different. We have had different experiences that have shaped us and formed our thinking and ways of being. But stripped of the body, the cultures we dwell in, and the minds with which we think, we are all soul, divine in origin and limitless in potential.

As I sat in the back seat of the car that night, little did I know that I was preparing to hear my own call. God was already calling my name.

In his essay, "Spiritual Law," Emerson wrote:

"Each man has his own vocation. The talent is the call. There is one direction in which all space is opened to him. He has faculties silently inviting him thither to endless exertion. He is like a ship in a river; he runs against obstructions on every side but one; on that side all obstruction is taken away, and he sweeps serenely over a deepening channel into an infinite sea."

My call to the vocation of healing came in a dream. In 1989 I had returned to school to renew my teaching certificate. I had spent many years working in the health food industry, and although

I had found a passionate interest in all fields relating to health and nutrition, I thought it was time to return to my original field of teaching.

Then one night I had the following experience in the dream state. A woman was instructing me in foot reflexology. She and I were seated in front of a reclining chair. An endless parade of people took turns sitting in the chair to receive the treatment and the visual diagnosis the woman was teaching me. Occasionally a man would enter the room, observe our progress, and then leave. This experience seemed to go on for most of the night. I now recognize the two beings in my dream experience as two of my spiritual guides who have been with me all of my life, guiding me through major turning points.

When I awoke, I passionately wanted to learn what I had been doing on the inner. A fire had been lit within me. Where to begin? It seemed reasonable to start with a course in foot reflexology.

I began making phone calls that very day, trying to locate a school where I might study. At that time there were no reflexologists in my area. I called a massage therapist I knew, and she happened to have a brochure from an institute that traveled to major cities and taught its seminars to interested people. I phoned the school and received their schedule. In two weeks I was traveling to my first reflexology seminar. Needless to say, as I was driving away from home, having already dropped the education classes I was taking for teacher re-certification, I was seized with doubts and fears.

I had almost completed my studies. Why was I traveling to another city to meet with a group of strangers to study a technique completely foreign to me? Yet, I felt I must see this through.

The weekend was discouraging. My fingers, unaccustomed to the pressure and exertion required in the work, became very sore. I had difficulty remembering the instructions and understanding the philosophy. I felt as if I were in a foreign country. When I returned home, I tried to practice my technique for the second seminar, which would be held two weeks later. I had to use the book to remind me of the steps, and still had difficulty getting my fingers and thumbs to work in the right way. It had seemed so simple in the dream!

In the second class, I fared somewhat better. I was still a long way from being proficient and having the necessary strength in my hands. But a miracle happened in my third seminar. I just suddenly had it! My inner and outer worlds merged. The instructor walked by the table where I was working. "How long have you been doing this?" he asked. "A month," I replied. "A month!" was his incredulous response. I took that to mean I was doing o.k.

After more classes and more practice, I was finally ready to see clients. At last the reward was at hand. I was so pleased with myself. I had followed my inner guidance, persevered, and now I was ready to begin a new career. Little did I know that Spirit had further plans for me, and that I was at the beginning stages, the most elementary stages, of my training. My study at the institute was nearing an end, but my real training in the art and science of healing was just beginning.

Soon after I began to work as a reflexologist, I began to receive strong inner nudges to add something to the end of the treatment. I was instructed to place my hands flat against the bottoms of the feet and hold them there. The first time I did this, I felt a kind of electrical energy move from my hands into the person's feet. I quickly put an end to that! I had heard all of the warnings about dabbling in psychic healing and the dangers of intruding into someone's personal space. I wanted no part of whatever was trying to come through me. However, it was extremely persistent, and I tentatively tried holding the feet for a few moments at the end of the sessions to see what the effect would be. (You have to understand that I was probably the first reflexologist in the city, and I didn't know of anyone who was doing energy healing at that time.)

At first while holding the feet, I would chat with the clients so that they would think I was just pausing a moment and wouldn't think I was doing anything strange. Over the course of the next several days, I was given three more holding positions for the feet to be added at the end of the sessions. I noticed that when I began this series of positions, the clients automatically closed their eyes and either fell asleep or sometimes went out of the body. It was . during this brief time at the end of the session where the miracles of healing took place. Though I didn't know what I was doing or · how it worked, I knew that something profound was taking place.

I watched peace settle into worried hearts and anger and other imbalanced emotions transform into love and gratitude. "Benediction"
was the word one woman used to describe her experience.

This was all wonderful, but I wanted to know what I was doing
and how it worked. I had a dream that told me that the four positions on the feet related to the four directions of the medicine
wheel, or wheel of life of ancient cultures. The wheel of life represents soul's journey through the cycles of life. The four positions,
I was told, also related to the four basic elements of creation—earth,
water, fire and air. I learned that, when the four elements and the
organs they control are in balance, the person experiences good
physical and emotional health.

My inner training continued as I learned other ways to energet-
ically clear congested areas in the body through the feet. Since the
feet are a map of the body, I learned much about the body's energy
zones and how all parts are related and affect each other. But soon I
was dissatisfied with the level of help I was able to provide. I knew
that in the cases of severe illness that I was seeing, the emotions
and spirit were involved in the illness, and that the cure must come
from within. I looked at different options available in furthering my
training. Everything proved to be a dead end.

Spirit seemed to be telling me to wait. More was to come.

One morning I was at home watching what was then a brand
new channel, the Discovery Channel, on television. The program
was on Qi Gong, an ancient Chinese method of healing. Now you
can attend classes on Qi Gong in most cities, but at that time it was
relatively unknown in the United States. The program showed the
Chi Masters working in hospitals in China, treating a roomful of
the most ill patients at the same time by projecting chi from their
hands toward the patients. "Now that is what I need to be able to
do," I thought. I could help many more people much more quickly
if I had those skills! But I certainly couldn't travel to China, and if
I did, how could I convince one of those Masters to teach me, and it
would take years. I did call the new age bookstore in town, and they
had one book on the subject. But it only had a couple of paragraphs
describing the external chi healing I had seen on the TV show. The
rest of the book was devoted to breathing and movement exercises.
I soon forgot about this mysterious form of healing.

A few months later a powerful new energy suddenly just turned on in my hands. It happened one evening. It was uncomfortable. I didn't know what to do with it or what to make of what was happening. I went outside and walked around. Finally I decided to go into contemplation and ask for guidance. "Pick up your hands," a quiet voice said. I raised my arms, and the energy shot from my hands in a powerful stream. "Well, you asked to learn Qi Gong!" was the only response from the voice.

I was flooded with amazement and gratitude and wonder. In that moment I knew I was guided, loved, and assisted in ways that I could never have dreamed. An ability that could have taken twenty years to master was just given to me, a supreme act of grace. What did it all mean? How was I supposed to use this new gift? What would people think? Always, always, that thought was in the back of my mind. What would people think?

I have since learned to trust the ways of the Holy Spirit, and to overcome many of my fears of the unknown. At that time, however, each step was a huge test of acceptance and surrender.

I experimented with a few close friends and clients who were open-minded. We found that indeed the external healing seemed to treat the entire body at once and brought an even deeper relaxation. Still, the doubts plagued me. I was being taken deeper into a world of energy that I didn't have the experience or knowledge to understand.

There was no one I could ask. There were very few people with whom I could share my inner experiences. I especially didn't want to get off track spiritually. My connection to Spirit was my lifeline, my source, my joy, my purpose. I wanted to make sure I wasn't being led into psychic abilities that could harm others or me. I needed a sign that I was going in the right direction.

One day as a friend and I were going to lunch, I noticed something in the road beside the car. "Look," I said. "It is a medal off of someone's uniform." I reached down and picked it up. It was a small medal on a ribbon. On one side was an open hand; the other bore the words: "Humanitarian Service Award."

I knew this was my sign from the Holy Spirit that my work was a service to humanity. I felt grateful in my lonely journey of discovery.

In 1994 a friend and I opened the first Center. It was time to bring this healing work, which I had named Directional Healing, to the public in a more open way. I had been told that it was time to "drop the feet," meaning drop the reflexology, and convert the system that I had learned to a complete energy healing system. Changes continued to come quickly.

One night I was doing some external healing for a friend, hands in the raised position, and the voice spoke and said, "Put down your hands." I dropped my hands to my lap, and the energy shot from my third eye, or sixth chakra. She opened her eyes. "What did you do!" she exclaimed. She had felt the energy change to a more powerful flow. One day after that experience while I was working with a client, the energy, on its own volition, flowed from my third eye in a beam of blue light. "God's breath," were the words I heard reverently spoken by an inner voice. I knew that the woman on the table was receiving deep mental and emotional healing, and I was receiving at the same time more confirmation that the ever-changing work was aligned with my spiritual goals. God was breathing through me.

By this time I was teaching the work to others. We had now begun to enter the process of healing through resonance. In other words, the healing was being done through a process of inner attunement through resonance. The healing practitioner, as the instrument of healing, resonates the healing frequencies through his or her entire being, tuning the physical body and inner states of being of the client. The healing practitioner is only the instrument. The frequencies, the experiences, the outcome, are all determined at a very high level beyond the scope and human abilities of the healer. Only Spirit can heal.

A dramatic change happened a couple of years later. I entered a state of being that I could only describe as a spiritual crisis, a dark night of soul. I felt deeply uprooted and emotionally and spiritually devastated. I cried all of the time. Doubts filled my being. Who was I, and what was I doing? At the same time, waves of energy were constantly washing through me, adjusting and preparing me for what was to come. It seemed that I had to "come undone" and be arranged in a new order of being to go further with the work. I began to hear a little refrain playing inside of me: "It's all about

Soul. It's all about Soul." I told my co-workers that a big change was coming, and that somehow it was about soul.

One day I knew it was time to give birth to this new level of energy. I called together a group of trusted practitioners who had been with me the longest. We went into contemplation, and an energetic process began that lasted about an hour. All of the turmoil, confusion, and suffering of the previous months melted as this new energetic way of being opened within us. The truths of healing that were imparted to us that day remain in the silent chambers of our own hearts. We knew that the direction of healing had been changed that day, for us and through us.

I will not attempt to describe to you the many changes that have continued, and will continue, in my work. The purpose of sharing these experiences is to show a little of how the co-creative process works, and the wondrous things that can happen when we follow our hearts and the inner voice that guides us, despite the fears we may have about how society might judge us. When Catherine Marshall received the inner guidance to write her husband's autobiography after his death, she was told that the story was important only in that it showed how God worked in this one man's life. The book touched many lives, including my own.

We always think that extraordinary things happen to extraordinary people, the people we see on television or read about in books. Extraordinary things, miraculous things, happen in the lives of people who learn the art of listening to the voice of God, and then follow that guidance, and the song in their own hearts, in spite of their fears or feelings of inadequacy. Our current level of ability, our current circumstances in life, do not limit divine grace. But rather divine grace tempers our abilities and circumstances. God does not call the equipped. He equips the called.

Chapter 2

Waking Up to God's Love

Have you ever thought about how many of our myths and legends deal with awakening from a sleep, from stories of sleeping princesses to sleeping giants and dragons? Life in a physical existence, unless soul is awakened and operating through the consciousness, is like being asleep. We can spend an entire lifetime, or many lifetimes, believing that day-to-day existence is our only lot in life. We haven't yet awakened the true self within. Yet there is something that nags at us and causes discontent. We may try to stifle this discontent with more sleep, more food, more sex, or mood altering substances like alcohol or drugs. An old saying comes to mind, "Let sleeping dogs lie." Sleeping dogs don't cause any problems.

I caught part of an interview on television with an author who was discussing some controversial ideas in another writer's books. "Why do these books make people uncomfortable?" asked the interviewer. "Because most people are not comfortable with a heroic view of life," was the reply. Indeed, waking up to the full possibility and the full responsibility of our existence can be a daunting thing. Yet waking up is a necessary part of the healing journey.

We want something from life, but life also wants something from us. We want healing, help, guidance, and our rightful share of happiness. Spirit needs channels, co-workers. It wants to express through us, to manifest Itself through our lives. It is easy to look at a sculpture or painting, or listen to Mozart, and say, "That person was an instrument of God." But we can't see how we could be instruments of the divine in our mundane lives. Yet we are. Every time we exhibit one of the qualities of God —compassion, patience, unconditional love — we are making ourselves, and life around us, more God-like.

A few years ago a woman in another state took one of my healing classes. She expressed her feelings of unworthiness and doubted her ability to work as a healing practitioner. When the second class approached, her doubts returned. She called me and told me she had considered dropping out of the study program, but then she had a dream that changed her mind. In the dream she was with a spiritual teacher. He asked her to give him the healing treatment she was learning. She felt very humbled and a little afraid to do the work on this spiritual being. As she prepared the table for the session, he said to her, "Connie, God doesn't have enough co-workers." She awoke with the realization that the Holy Spirit had sent this messenger to remind her that her desire was to be a co-worker with God, and her feelings of unworthiness were standing in her way.

I heard a woman on television describe how she turned her life around. She had been in great financial difficulty. She decided to start a small catering business, selling sandwiches at lunchtime at local businesses. From this small start, her business grew to a large catering operation. She then opened a restaurant that became very popular and successful. Her comment was: "Since the day I started helping myself, God hasn't stopped blessing me. God helps those who help themselves."

Co-working implies that we have an important role to play in life. And God can only do for us what It can do through us.

There is one thing we need to understand, however. It has been my experience that God doesn't strike bargains. We may try to bargain with God in a moment of human desperation, but we cannot harness the power of Spirit to work for us. But when we learn the inner secret of aligning our will with It, It works with us. There is a paradox in the nature of Spirit. While the Holy Spirit is the agent of change, Spirit Itself is unchanging. It is we who must change. It is the eternal, sustaining, unifying force of all the universes. Its basic nature is the same today as it has been for eons of time. So our task is to learn to hear, to listen to, and to come into agreement with the Holy Spirit, the voice of God.

Coming into agreement with the voice of God means that God's will supersedes our own. We make our goals, state our desires, and then we say, "Thy will be done." It means surrendering our preconceived ideas about how things should be, what reality should look like. It means giving up our attachments, our needs, and our fears. It means, after doing our part, totally placing the outcome in God's hands. Coming into full agreement with the voice of God, the light and sound of God, means that the very atoms of our body will resonate with It's music, and our atoms will reflect It's light. At this point, we have become inseparable from It. Its will cannot be distinguished from our own, and we ourselves become the wondrous instruments of change.

I have observed that often an illness is the way that we learn something about ourselves and our relationship with the Holy Spirit. An illness can bring a lesson about cause and effect, an experience of humility and grace, and sometimes a miracle.

I began my spiritual quest in earnest in my mid-twenties. My new spiritual life often took me on out of town trips to seminars or workshops. Some trips were to provide a service or assistance to others. On one such occasion, I had agreed to travel to the southern part of the state to meet with a man in a V.A. hospital. Shortly before the trip was to take place, I developed a slipped disc in my back, a very painful condition. I was seeing my doctor several times a week. I told him I needed to make this trip. He said, "It will hurt you. At least get out of the car and walk around frequently."

Just as he promised, the trip was uncomfortable. But the meeting with the gentleman in the hospital was wonderful. He spoke about his wife. The family had very little, and his wife couldn't read or write. But he said that he read to her from spiritual books, and she had a true and deep love for God and for life. She had a rich inner life of incredible spiritual experiences. There was a special light and love within this man. He had gifts that money couldn't buy. Meeting this humble, gentle man had been a blessing. I had gone there to assist him, but I felt I had received more than I had given.

Also, by the time I returned home, my back had completely healed! I went to my doctor and told him. He said, "It does happen sometimes." He said he was relieved for me, for he knew I had been facing many months of therapy and discomfort.

The interesting point, now that I look back, is that it never occurred to me to ask for spiritual assistance with the journey. Nor did I ask for a healing. I simply felt a spiritual need to honor my agreement. The solution existed without the question being asked.

Often it is our constant questioning and worrying that separates us from the very answers we seek. Questioning, worrying, pushing, creates tension. Tension and worry close us off from contact with Spirit. A relaxed, receptive inner attitude is needed to make contact with the spiritual forces.

Around that same time I went though a period of experiencing angina attacks. It is frightening to experience chest pains and to have difficulty breathing. I was out of town one weekend when one of these episodes happened. That night, able to take only shallow breaths because of the pain, I eventually fell asleep. During the night, my spiritual guide at that time appeared by my side. He gently took my hand and said, "I love you." With that utterance of divine love, my pain vanished.

These two situations and others that followed were spiritual wake-up calls for me. I later came to know that my spirit was trying to get my attention through my body. Even though I was young and for the most part healthy, my spirit was deeply wounded. A deeper part of me was crying for healing. That is why, once one problem would be taken care of, a few months or maybe a few years later, another one would surface.

For most of us waking up must be a gradual process, unless God taps you on the shoulder and needs you for a specific task. Such was the case of Saul of Tarsus. As a Roman, Saul was not a friend to the Jews. Yet God had a mission for him — to bring the message of love and the open heart taught by Jesus to the Gentiles. One day on the road to Damascus, Saul had an experience with the light and sound of God. The light left him temporarily blind so that he could gain a new spiritual vision, and the sound conveyed his mission. Saul, a new man, became Paul, and took up his work of traveling and teaching and writing about the Christian doctrine.

Our spiritual wake- up calls can be almost as dramatic. A wake-up call is usually a major turning point and may center around a major life change such as a divorce, a serious illness, the death of a loved one, or loss of a job.

When I was in my early thirties, I became very ill. I was a single parent and had to work to support my daughter and myself. Yet my illness was making it difficult to do the smallest details of daily life. With no health insurance and little money, I knew it was up to me to turn my condition around. I sought spiritual guidance from my dreams and contemplations. I received guidance to begin a certain dietary program. At first I resisted this idea. It represented such a dramatic change in cooking and eating. I would have to teach myself this system, and it seemed very foreign to me. Yet each time I picked up a book and began to read about it, my heart center would feel warm and open.

My mind continued to argue with me for a while. The mind doesn't like change, since it runs in grooves and patterns like a well-worn record. To recover I had to do something different. Once I made the commitment to become well and learn this new way of eating, I found it to be an exciting adventure with many rewards. I continued the program for three and a half years, and I learned so much about the power of foods to heal. I developed a great respect for the plant kingdom and gratitude for the life and energy that whole foods bring us. My intuition became keener, and I was becoming stronger. I had found within myself a strength and a will that was more powerful than my illness. I look back now, and I know that the strength was love. Not a love for my body or an attachment to my physical existence, but a love that was something deeper, more permanent, and had always been with me.

Now we are getting close to the secret of healing. It is always love that heals.

Although my body was stronger, my spirit was far from being healed and whole. My new state of physical health made it possible for my spirit to awaken a little more. I began to realize that there was much that I didn't know about myself. We all have private corners within ourselves that are hidden from the world, yet haunt us by their presence. Unexplained fears or aversions, unprovoked feelings of anger, self-loathing and anxieties are some of the ways these unexamined parts of ourselves surface. I suddenly found myself occasionally experiencing very strong feelings of grief, but from an unknown source. I would turn on the shower and sob as if I would never reach the end of the crying, or sit outside by myself at night and cry, feeling deep anguish that I couldn't understand. I developed chest pains and an irregular heartbeat. I knew that my body and my consciousness were at war. My consciousness knew the truth. My body was trying to suppress it.

Through a series of dreams and a growing inner awareness, I began to suspect that I had been sexually abused by my father. He and my mother separated when I was seven, and I didn't remember much about our life with him. One day I was driving back home from a short trip, feeling quite happy and enjoying the beautiful day and the open road. My attention was suddenly drawn to the radio. The news had come on, and the reporter was talking about the growing problem of disposal of hospital waste. A bomb exploded in my consciousness. I suddenly remembered the abuse. The knowledge and memory washed over me like an acid bath.

The word hospital triggered the opening of the door in my unconscious. I remembered how afraid of doctors and hospitals I had been as a child. I was terrified that I would have to go to the hospital. I felt that they would hurt me by putting something inside of me. Then I remembered that my father had initiated the abuse by saying, "Let's play doctor."

When I got home, I felt as if my whole world had shifted. My life had been lived under an illusion. At least now I knew I wasn't crazy, and I could begin releasing the mess I had carried around inside of me for all of those years. I was looking forward to feeling normal and releasing the secret shame I had always felt. There was no place for those feelings in the life I now had and in the spiritual journey I was pursuing.

Healing of trauma takes its own time and comes in stages. I had no desire to claim the right to be treated as a victim. I knew that the victim consciousness carried a very high price, trapping one in a cycle of inertia and introversion in return for a very small payoff — sympathy or the right to an excuse for not succeeding or being happy.

My final healing and release of the effects of the abuse came shortly after my Mother's death several years later. She was too old and too frail to ever discuss this with her, and it would have served no purpose. I truly felt she had no conscious memory of it, and it would have shattered her. A couple of months after her death, my son and daughter and I went on a weekend trip that took us through my old hometown. I wanted to drive by the house where I had grown up. As I stood in front of the house, my lower back began to hurt. As I drove home, the pain became more and more severe. By the time we reached home, I could barely move.

A few days later when the inflammation had subsided a bit, I went to a chiropractor who used a non-force method of adjustment to see if that would speed my recovery. I lay face down on his table and turned my head to the left. A bookcase was directly in front of me. Incredibly, *Let's Play Doctor* was the title my eyes fastened on. I stood up and said, "I'm sorry. I have to leave." I sat in the car in the parking lot and cried.

I was weary in spirit and body, yet so keenly aware of the blessing and the miracle I had just experienced. Spirit had just given me the confirmation that my healing was being completed. The trauma in my back was the original trauma from the abuse being released from the places it had been stored. My Mother was no longer here. I didn't have to protect her any longer. It was safe to let it all go. My back healed quickly. I marveled at how my higher consciousness and Spirit had so meticulously navigated the entire healing experience very gradually over the period of several years, allowing me to take small steps in acceptance, each step bringing more freedom and love.

Before my Mother died, she was in a nursing home for several months. One night when I went to visit her, a new roommate had been moved into the room with her. Pam was a young woman in her thirties who had been paralyzed in a car accident several years before. She couldn't speak and had very limited movement. She could move one arm. She communicated by laboriously moving her hand across an alphabet board someone had constructed for her. This was a very slow process since she had to spell out each word one letter at a time with a hand that was partially crippled.

The first night I met Pam she was very frightened and was moaning in deep despair, drooling and flailing the one arm helplessly. I didn't know anything about her at that point and didn't know if she might be mentally impaired. I just knew that seeing her condition was more than my heart could bear in that moment. I cried all the way home for her and for the world. "There is just so much need, and I am so small," was my cry to God. I knew I was going through a time of being stretched to be able to accept and to give more of God's love. I could sense the enormity of the love, yet I felt so very small.

Pam was soon moved to another room, but I continued to visit with her every day when I went to see Mother. One day when I went in, she was moaning and very upset. I couldn't understand what she was trying to communicate to me. Finally she grabbed my hand and was trying to place it on her head. Then she began to spell "pray." My heart surged with compassion for this young woman's suffering. I said with all of the earnestness within me, "Pam, God has not forgotten you. I think it is time for you to have your own angel to help you." I went out on a spiritual limb and said, "I promise you that tonight a special spiritual being will come to you to help you."

The next day when I returned, she broke into a smile when I entered the room. I asked her if she had had a visitor the night before. She pointed to " yes" on her board. Pam began to have regular spiritual experiences and was being taught by her special spiritual guide and friend. I looked forward to hearing of her adventures. She began to tell me more of her history, and thoughts and fears. Pam was waking up.

One day I went in and she was again in deep anguish. "I know what is wrong," she spelled out. "I am paralyzed." She let out a deep moan with this pronouncement. I was astounded. How could she have lived in this condition all of these years and not been aware of her plight? I suddenly realized that her consciousness had constructed some kind of delusional state and denial for her as a survival mechanism; otherwise she would not have been able to cope with her situation. Pam was growing spiritually, but the price was high. She had to be awake in order to grow. But being awake also meant waking up to a full awareness of her condition.

God was teaching me so much through Pam. The desire to live is strong even in the most dire circumstances. The human spirit is amazing in its capacity to adapt and survive. And love and gratitude can flourish even in the most wounded hearts.

Pam's injuries were on the outside and fully evident to everyone except herself. For most of us they are deeply hidden inside, yet still cause spiritual paralysis and keep us from being fully alive.

We carry within us traumas, not only from our childhoods, but also from other lifetimes. The unconscious memories are not there to give us the excuse to become a suffering victim, to suffer because we were treated wrongly. They are there to help us unfold spiritually, to teach us something about love, forgiveness, and acceptance.

Other illnesses and problems come because we break the laws of life. Unconscious behavior sooner or later catches up with us. We carelessly continue behaviors, whether it is how we eat, think, or treat others, that harm us. How else do we learn except by hard experience?

Therefore to invite healing is to invite change, and when we do, our healing journey begins. Not just a physical healing of our ailments, but a healing and releasing of the inner ills that keep us from a full life of freedom, joy and love--the freedom to experience life, not as a burden, not as a series of tragic events to be endured, but as a gift. Life is a gift.

Everyday can be a new beginning in life. In fact, every moment can be the starting point for a new level of experience. Our attempts at creating change fail when we use as our starting point our old patterns of limitation and belief. We cannot start from a position of limitation and expect to succeed. So we must take as our starting point the one creative, limitless force in the universe. Instead of attempting to impress our ideas on the substance of Spirit and mold it to fill our wishes and desires, we can invite Spirit to infuse our minds and hearts with the appropriate ideas, goals, and dreams.

This is the path of least resistance. We cease fighting life, trying to wrench from it our rightful share of good things. Instead we come into a realization of oneness with the substance of life, that which supplies all things. This is the supreme creative act—we have aligned with flow.

Through this inner alignment, not only are our own needs met, but we also become a source of supply for others. We are learning how to become a co-worker with God.

If I hadn't learned to pay attention to my dreams as a source of inner guidance, my path in life would have been very different. I would have continued with the education classes, perhaps found a teaching job, perhaps not. But I would have continued on a course set by my mind based on past experience, simply because I didn't have the capacity to imagine all of the events that followed the dream in 1989. Spirit can suggest a course for us that not only fulfills us and creates genuine growth, it provides a way for continued expansion of ourselves and those around us. It is the principle of increase. Once we know this, it would be foolish to limit ourselves to only what we know or can currently imagine. We haven't begun to tap the full resources of Spirit. When our imaginations are freed from convention and fear, anything is possible.

Chapter 3

The Creative Power of Love

My daughter was born in 1975. When I went home from the hospital with this little newborn, I forgot everything I had learned about life up to that point. It was a new life infused with a new love. I also found myself with the luxury of time. My days were spent holding, nursing, and rocking this precious infant. This newfound love recreated me, and I took advantage of these days to explore this new state of being. I knew that in this child I was meeting one of my life partners, and that she would be my teacher, my child, my friend, and that I would always love her, no matter what.

I had time to read, to contemplate. I existed in a cocoon of love and comfort. One morning while she was sleeping, I read for a while and then entered contemplation. Suddenly, I found myself above my body. I remember having the realization: "I am a cone of energy." I was experiencing myself as energy with a viewpoint, simply a vibrational state of awareness. I knew that I was soul, and that I had a body.

This experience of myself as soul left me in an elevated state of awareness for days. I floated through each day in a state of bliss. Gradually, the human state of consciousness crept back in as the daily events of life pulled me back into everyday reality. This new, profound love for my child had opened my heart wider, allowing me to go beyond myself.

Now I know, many years later, that our spiritual purpose is to learn how to live in that elevated awareness, from the viewpoint of soul, every day. It is possible to experience life as a higher reality than that provided by our physical senses. The way to bridge the inner and outer parts of our being is through contemplation, meditation, or prayer. And, as illustrated in my story, an open, loving heart is the key.

Animals also teach us a lot about love. My experiences with dogs began when I was a toddler. I am told that when I was a young child, whenever the front door was opened, I took off running down the street. (I don't know where I was going, except that, even then, I was looking for freedom.) We had a Collie named Penny. Penny would chase after me, grab my dress in her mouth, and pull me back home. Penny knew I wasn't ready for that much freedom. She was a loving guardian, providing safety for a determined child.

There are other guardians that have been with us throughout our lives. Once I re-experienced the major turning points in my life in a contemplative experience. In the contemplative state, however, I was allowed to see the experiences from a larger perspective, and to see that my spiritual teachers and guides had been there all along. Never had I been alone. I didn't have the awareness to sense their presence and help during the earlier stages of my life.

An important part of inviting healing is to invite spiritual help. Ask God to send your teacher, or to make your guide known to you. Inner guidance can come in a dream, a strong inner feeling or nudge, or can even be in a written or spoken message that stands out and gets your attention. For example, you might be riding in your car and spot a billboard or a bumper sticker that has a message that is meaningful to you in your current circumstances. When a person has an experience with an audible spiritual voice, and receives inner guidance that way, he is hearing one of God's messengers. (Not to be confused with the voices of mental illness or psychic entities.) A spiritual voice will never ask you to harm yourself or others. The message is always one of love, reassurance, and upliftment. And the messages are usually infrequent and brief. They want us to learn to think for ourselves, to develop our own spiritual mastery.

Sometimes we have gone as far as a particular teacher can take us, and it is time to take the next step spiritually. A guide or teacher will turn us over to the next teacher, just as a schoolteacher promotes a student to the next grade. There is no competition among these spiritual beings. They are true co-workers with God. Their only mission is to serve.

If you would like, you can ask the Holy Spirit to create a special Spiritual Advisory Team to assist you as you go through the remaining process of this book. In the inner worlds there are spiritual specialists of every kind. There are temples where you can go to study or for healing. Before going to sleep at night, ask your guide to take you to a place of healing, or to a temple to learn a new skill that you would like to develop. Be sure to record your dreams for clues about your inner journey, or for insights into steps you need to take on the outer to complete your healing or improve your life.

During your daytime contemplation, invite your special guides to help you. Look for God's inner light and listen for the inner sound, the voice of Spirit. This time spent in contemplation will strengthen you, and give you clarity and renewed purpose. Experiences with the light and sound purify us, gradually replacing negative states within us with more love and contentment. Later in the book you will be given examples of contemplation exercises. The main thing is to approach this sacred time with love and gratitude.

Our guides can help us with our spiritual mission. About two years before I began writing this book, my teacher told me in a dream that "the book is important." I understood that at some point I would write about healing. I left the timing and the details to Spirit.

Then one summer I suddenly found myself at home with very few clients calling in for appointments. Then my left thumb became so inflamed that I could no longer do sessions for the regular clients that remained. I began to wonder if I was supposed to close the Center and look for a regular job. I kept feeling that I needed to wait, that something was in the process of unfolding. I knew it was the perfect time to be writing, since I had so much free time. But I didn't really know what direction to take.

Then one morning I awoke with the idea for this book. A few days later, information for two chapters began to flow through my awareness. A week later, more information came that provided the bridge for those two parts. I spent that evening reading, contemplating, and preparing inwardly. The next morning I arose early and began to write. I wrote every day after that for six to eight hours a day until that section was completed. My finances, my health, everything seemed inconsequential except the desire to let this work come through me. A vortex of energy had opened above and within me, and the information was simply flowing through me and into the computer.

One chapter came through the dream state. One morning I awoke before dawn hearing a voice speaking to me. The last phrases of the inner dialogue were trailing off as I came to awareness. I knew that while I was asleep, I had been receiving information for an important chapter. I could only consciously remember one phrase—sympathetic vibratory response. How in the world was I going to reconstruct the inner message? But I had confidence that my awareness knew the content for the chapter. I sat down at the computer, and after a halting beginning, the chapter flowed as effortlessly as the rest of the chapters had.

I contemplated the process of being a co-worker, and the co-creative process. One thing was clear—the information was coming through me and not from me. Whether or not it was from soul, the knowing part of me, or directly from the Holy Spirit, I cannot say for sure. But I also was aware that the spiritual force at work had to use what I was—it took the experiences and stories from my own life and wove them into the spiritual principles that were being discussed. The Holy Spirit, using the law of economy, is going to work along the lines of least resistance. It is not going to compose a symphony through me, nor am I likely to stun the world of science with a new invention. But through me it could write about love and healing. It had spent years preparing me.

At the close of the writing experience, I felt waves of love washing over me. I knew it was God's love for the individuals who would read the book. When we use our creative abilities with love and sincerity, whether it is to cook a meal, arrange flowers, or make music or art, we add love and healing in some mysterious way to the whole of things. We are manifesting God.

Chapter 4

The Most Powerful Prayer

We think that we should pray for what we need, but saying thank you for what we already have is actually the most powerful prayer. Gratitude is a powerful creative force.

I remember learning to recite a simple prayer when I was a child that ended with these two lines: "Thank you for the birds that sing; thank you, God, for everything." Each morning during my time of reading and contemplation, I try to recapture that innocent childlike wonder and gratefulness. Thank you, God, for everything.

Last year a phrase from a poem by Gerard Manley Hopkins, "Pied Beauty," kept going through my mind. I hadn't thought of this poem in years, and suddenly this one line was constantly in my thoughts: "Glory be to God for dappled things." I modified the phrase to, "Thank you, God, for dappled things." It became a mantra for me. I thought perhaps it was a reminder to be aware of the beauty in all of creation.

At that time I was also involved in an earnest search for a dog. I had seen a dog in a dream. It was a somewhat large dog, some kind of hound, I thought. I knew she was very sensitive, and that I loved her very much. So I began to wonder about this dog, and if I would indeed find her. One day I was in the pet store buying cat food, and a woman from out of town who is involved in greyhound rescue was in the store with two of the rescued dogs. I had never seen a greyhound, but something drew me to these exotic, strangely quiet and serene dogs.

I began to have more dreams about dogs. This time they clearly were greyhounds. Then I suddenly began to see greyhounds everywhere. I saw them in television ads, in the pet store, passing by in cars. A dog I had never seen before in my life was suddenly everywhere. A great longing began to grow in me to find my "dream dog."

I read everything I could about the breed. I researched the greyhound adoption sites on the Internet. I filled out applications. No one seemed to have a dog under sixty pounds. (My apartment complex had a weight limit on pets.) I seemed to have reached a dead end. I had done all I could do, and I left it in the hands of Spirit. Then one evening I got a call from an organization saying they had some small greyhounds that they thought might fit my requirements.

I anxiously drove to the nearby town the next day, hopeful that one of these dogs would be the dog in my dreams. "Will I recognize her?" I wondered. The first dog they brought out for me was a forty-nine pound brindle female—one of God's dappled things!

I realized I had been giving thanks for the gift of this animal friend who was already on her way to me. My soul already knew her, and was grateful for this gift of love.

I believe that this continual gratitude prayer helped lead me to my dog. As I drove home with her after months of searching and longing to meet this special companion, my heart fairly burst with love. I told one friend that I felt as if I had won the lottery.

When we establish a goal or dream for ourselves, we can begin to express gratitude for it, knowing it is already on its way to us. This is thinking from the end. Our hearts and minds are filled with the feeling of the dream realized. Gratitude is the natural response. Giving daily thanks in advance demonstrates confidence that our good is on its way to us. The process works as if by magic when we are truly grateful.

A prayer of gratefulness is the most powerful prayer we can utter. Another word for gratitude is appreciation. To appreciate means to increase in value. To depreciate is to decrease in value. To put the principle of increase into effect in our lives, we can practice being grateful. To have an attitude of entitlement, to take for granted, to fail to appreciate people, things, or the gifts of life, is the sure way to limit growth, prosperity, and healing. When we demean and devalue our lives with complaints or a sense of entitlement, we close off the natural flow of life.

A friend of mine named Kathy is a college instructor. One weekend she had to give up her Saturday to attend an all day conference at the university. She would rather have been at home with her family. She decided to make the most of the day by adopting an attitude of gratefulness.

She was a little late for the conference, since she had attended another meeting first. The person at the registration desk told her not to bother paying the registration fee, since she had missed part of the program. Then the woman said, "But that means you will miss lunch, since it is included in the registration fee." Kathy had eaten a late breakfast; so she didn't mind. After lunch, the woman said that there were several box lunches left over, and offered Kathy one. Then when the door prize was given away, Kathy won. She won a valuable $90.00 book! She was certain that deciding to make the best of the day by having an attitude of appreciation had brought all of this good fortune to her.

Tom, another friend, decided he wanted to become a more grateful person. Every day he practiced being grateful for even the smallest thing. Gratitude became a regular part of his spiritual practice and life. About a year later, his company had an employee luncheon. The highlight of the event was a drawing for a special prize the company was giving away as an employee appreciation gift. Tom was sitting quietly, feeling grateful for the turkey sandwich on his plate, when his co-workers told him he had won the drawing. Tom thought they were playing a joke on him. But sure enough, Tom's name had been drawn. He was the winner of a brand new BMW automobile!

Tom's car was very old. He needed a new car. And besides that, Tom had never owned a new car. He had always driven used ones. Tom had not asked the Holy Spirit for a new car. He had asked for a more grateful heart. The Holy Spirit knew that Tom needed a car, and that he was the person in the room who would appreciate the car the most.

All of these stories illustrate an important secret of creativity and manifestation. We can focus attention on a quality or principle, rather than on acquiring a particular thing. The realization of the principle brings into manifestation the corresponding things.

Gratitude is the most powerful prayer. It opens us to receive the gifts of life. But an attitude of gratefulness also helps when the adventure of life brings an unexpected gift—the gift of change.

Chapter 5

Healing Through Change

To invite healing into our lives is to invite change. The end product of change is desirable. We envision better health and fitness, a loving partner, or financial abundance. But many times we don't realistically face the requirements of change.

We want change to happen the way it does in fairytales — the genie appears and gives us three wishes. The good news is that we actually get more than three wishes, and the genie lives inside us! How do we unleash the power of the genie? And what are the requirements of change?

The genie is the untapped creative powers of soul. A couple of years ago, I had a dream that illustrates this principle. In the dream I was walking through the neighborhood and saw that a vacant house had been renovated for a new business occupant. I had seen the house before, and noticed that it was very narrow. On this occasion, the front and back doors were open, and I could see all the way through the house. Since the door was open, I decided to go inside. I found that it was a business called "Make a Wish-Wishes Come True." A business card stated that, for a small fee, you could have a thirty-minute meeting with the wish master to discuss your wishes. I twirled around the room, singing out a wish that was in my heart.

When I awoke, I contemplated the meaning of this wonderful dream. I realized that the house was my consciousness. It could be entered by more than one way, or door. The opened doors indicated the consciousness was open and ready to accept change. The narrowness of the house represented the "narrow way" of the spiritual path. I thought of the Bible verse that says, "... strait is the gait, and narrow is the way...." (Matthew 7:14). The thirty minutes related to the time I spend in daily contemplation. The wish master represented soul, which contacts Spirit, the unconditioned substance of life, through contemplation. This responsive substance of life is shaped through the creative power of soul. Hence, our wishes are fulfilled by the Holy Spirit through the gateway of our own consciousness.

I wondered why the word "wish" was prominent in the dream. Then I realized that wishes represent our dreams. Dreams are the wishes our hearts make. A heartfelt dream or wish carries a creative power that is absent in analytical thought. Our strong feeling helps to manifest our desire.

The power, beauty, grace, wisdom, and freedom of soul can be unleashed in our lives. An experience with my greyhound, Gina, was a lesson about unleashing soul. I call this kind of experience a waking dream, because, as some nighttime dreams do, a waking dream brings awareness about a situation or a truth in life. Important dreams and waking dreams may repeat, as soul is trying to get an important message to our awareness.

This particular experience was telling me something about soul. I always walk Gina on a leash, knowing that I can't run nearly fast enough to catch up to a racing greyhound, should she decide to run off. One day we were out walking, and the leash suddenly just fell to the ground. Gina hardly noticed, and I was able to grab the leash and refasten it. I wondered how it could have come undone. I knew I had fastened it to the ring on the collar the way that I always do.

A few days later, the same thing happened. The leash dropped to the ground. This time Gina noticed, and she grabbed the leash in her mouth and walked holding the leash. She was so accustomed to being on the end of the leash that she just picked it up and continued walking. Since this had now happened twice, I examined the collar, ring, and leash more carefully. The spring mechanism in the hook wasn't broken. The ring was solid. Everything looked normal.

A few days later when we were out walking, the leash again fell to the ground. This time something clicked in Gina's awareness. She suddenly realized she was free. She took off running, as only a greyhound can. I could only hope that something would catch her attention and slow her down. Thankfully, a woman and a small white dog were walking down the street. Gina spotted them and raced towards them. She stopped to visit the dog and its owner, allowing me time to catch up with her.

I fastened Gina's leash and thanked the woman. As I walked Gina back toward the apartment, I wondered about this experience. Three separate occurrences were too many to be a coincidence. There was a message here. As I approached the door, the word freedom flashed in my mind. Later, I also realized that the experience represented the power of soul unleashed. I had been thinking about the things that bind us and hold us back, the "leashes" to which we are attached.

We are unaccustomed to true spiritual freedom, and when a little more freedom comes, in the form of an opportunity or new experience, we may grab the leash that makes us feel secure rather than trusting the new way being opened up for us.

For the full creative power of soul to be unleashed, we must be freed from the bindings of our own consciousness. No one imprisons us but ourselves. A movement toward change soon brings to our awareness the many fears, attachments, beliefs, and habits that create our world and circumstances.

We see ourselves as the victim of circumstances because we do not remember the cause that set events in motion. We are unconsciously living out the law of cause and effect. God gave soul the divine power of imagination, of creativity, so that we can experience greater life beyond our current circumstances.

We can choose to be cause, to consciously invite change, knowing that change is the doorway to progress. But since change is part of the principle of increase, change can go either way. If things are going badly, they can get worse. If they are going well, they can become even better. Change and increase are going to work from the starting point of our consciousness. So when we invite change, we want to align our plans for change with divine will, in whatever way is best for ourselves and for the good of the whole.

Sometimes things seem to get worse before they get better because there are some things within us that must be changed. This is sometimes referred to as a rechemicalization. Or it may be the little stores of karma working out so that we can move forward. In either case, it is sometimes a necessary part of transition.

Change is transition, transformation, and implies giving up something in order to receive something else. There are a few prin-

ciples that can help us identify what might be holding us back from
the change and healing we desire in our lives.

1. Motivation — What is our motivation for change, and how strong
   is our motivation for change? A small change might require only
   a small amount of motivation to accomplish our goal. A large
   change will require more. Our level of motivation must move
   from our heads to a deep connection with our hearts. Our action
   must spring from a passion that is grounded in our heart's desire.
   We will be motivated to work for what we deeply and sincerely
   want. A passing mental desire or whim is not strong enough to
   make real and lasting change.

2. Evaluation — We have to know where we are to determine
   where we want to go. An honest evaluation of our circumstances
   is necessary before we know what changes are needed. When
   we ask for healing and change to come into our lives, any form
   of denial must leave.

3. Knowledge — There are many ways to obtain knowledge about
   the change we want to make. Observation, research and study,
   and listening expand our awareness. Then, after we have made a
   sincere effort to gain the necessary knowledge, divine revelation
   provides the missing pieces through contemplation, a dream, or
   some other form of inner guidance.

4. Honesty — To know what is and is not working in our lives, we
   need to look at results. Being honest about our situation may
   mean we need to admit that we don't know everything, that
   we need to ask for help. Being honest may mean we need to
   overcome denial or a sense of pride and arrogance that is keeping
   us stuck. Pride and lack of humility can keep us from admitting
   the seriousness of our situation, or from asking for help or
   guidance.

5. Discipline — The willingness to carry out the necessary actions
   for change. If our goals are founded in our minds, it might take
   much mental discipline to keep us on track, and the discipline

is a chore. When our goals are linked to our heart's desire, the force of love propels us. We are enlivened by our dreams, and we will sacrifice whatever is necessary to manifest them. Love is the greatest motivator.

6. Determination — We must be willing to endure short-term discomfort for long-term benefit. Again, if we are in love with our ideal, determination naturally springs from within us to see the process through.

Now let's look at three reasons for change:
1. To experience health, happiness, and our share of abundance in life. These are rightful goals. They can, however, become sacred goals when we ask to be blessed in order to become a blessing to others. Our desires need to exceed the needs of the little self. How can my life bless others?
2. To be a better co-worker with God and life. We can be a servant of God no matter what our outer circumstances are. But if it is in the realm of physical and spiritual possibility to improve our condition, we owe it to life, to God, and to ourselves to do so. If we can accomplish more in life by undergoing change, then we can invite the change, or Spirit may thrust it upon us anyway.
3. To manifest our spiritual mission; to be the best that we can be.

In the above list, we moved in our goals from the personal to the universal. We began with our physical needs—the focus is on receiving. The second goal is serving—the focus is on giving. The third goal is to embody our spiritual ideal—the focus is on being.

Let's reverse the order and state our goals for change from the spiritual and universal downward to the personal:
1. My goal is to be the best that I can be, to align my outer life with soul's mission for this lifetime.
2. My goal is to be a co-worker with God, to manifest Its presence and qualities through my life.
3. My goal is to have the health and energy, proper relationships and employment that best enable me to further my spiritual goals. Thy will be done.

When we reordered the goals, the focus shifted into this order:
1. To embody our spiritual ideal. (Become one with the Source.)
2. Serving. (Become a source of supply.)
3. Improving our life and health. (Receiving our supply from our alignment, our oneness with the Source.)

This order of goals places primary importance on developing the spiritual consciousness. A spiritual consciousness in turn inspires service — the giving of ourselves out of love. The increase and expansion of consciousness provides the gateway to also fulfill our dreams for our physical life.

Specific goals and actions will spring out of these general goals. Our daily contemplation will fire our imaginations and fill our minds with plans. Remember, Soul has a plan for your life that is bigger than your mind can envision. Soul's plan can fill all of your dreams and some you haven't yet the capacity to dream. Soul's dream is eternal.

Regarding goal number three, the goals that relate to our physical needs--having spiritual goals does not mean that we need to ignore our personal needs. Remember that God is working through us. We are the instruments and need and deserve proper attention and care. The voice that has often provided inspiration and guidance in a time of need once said to me: "Susan, it is okay to ask for what you need." When a need is present, it is indeed okay to ask for help in filling that need.

In chapter three you were given the opportunity to form a Spiritual Advisory Team. Now that you will be considering your goals for healing and changing your life, you might find yourself being asked this question: "What do you want?"

Choose carefully. How you answer that question will greatly impact your life. Your answer will set in motion the forces of
. change.

Chapter 6

The Wisdom in Your Heart

Several years ago I had become despondent, tired of coping with the inner and outer demands of the work. The prospect of facing endless change that required deeper and deeper submission seemed overwhelming to me. Very simply, I was tired. One afternoon I was lying down, and that beloved inner voice whispered, ever so gently: "The majesty of the mission."

Instantly my despondency lifted. I felt elated. My human awareness needed the confirmation and reminder of what soul always knew: Soul's mission is majestic.

Your personal mission is no less majestic or important. The discontent, unhappiness, and lack of fulfillment you feel at times are the gnawing reminders that you came here to do and be more. Through the process of living, we may spend many years, many lifetimes, forgetting. It may be time to jostle the spiritual memory. It may be time to move more consciously toward your spiritual goals.

In your daily contemplation, begin by asking: "What did I come here to learn?" Write down your question, and then keep it lightly in your awareness as you go about your day. Repeat the question before you fall asleep at night. Make notes of the insights and answers that come.

When you feel ready, move to the next question: "What did I come here to do?" Let go of any preconceptions. The simplicity of the answers may surprise you.

When we ask something of Spirit, we must ask in a relaxed and gentle way, curious, trusting, and sincere. The more we push for an answer, the more the answer recedes. By asking in a relaxed way, we are opening the consciousness to receive knowledge that is already present within us.

When we make our goals for change, we need to leave room
for Spirit to modify them in whatever way may be best. If we
steadfastly hold to our original plan, we may miss many golden opportunities.

In 1989 when I decided I was ready for a job change, I made
plans to renew my teaching certificate so that I could return to
teaching. By making a plan and taking action, I set in motion the
forces of change. This allowed Spirit to enter the scene with a plan
that would best serve Its needs and also allow me to fulfill my own
spiritual agreements. I wanted to teach again, and I am teaching,
but I am teaching healing classes instead of high school English. I
wanted to continue researching and learning. The inner guidance
that enabled me to develop a new system of healing has opened a
world of inner research and revelatory learning that I could never
have imagined.

Place yourself in the position of needing information that isn't
available from any outer source, then you really discover how to
source what you need when you need it. You also discover that the
Holy Spirit is truly your co-worker. There are times when It seems
to leave us alone to our own devices. But It is merely giving us a
chance to try our spiritual wings, and to develop more self-mastery
and confidence in our relationship with It.

When I was taking the education classes that spring, I enrolled
in a class called Bibliotherapy. I was intrigued by the idea of literature as a therapeutic tool. It was the first time the class had been
offered. In the class we discussed how writing is therapeutic, and
we also discussed the healing images and messages in certain pieces
of literature. I didn't know it at the time, but this class was planting
within me the idea that the healing vibrations that would soon enter
my life could also be conveyed to others through my writing. The
Holy Spirit doesn't waste a single experience. It operates with an
economy of motion and effort. All has meaning.

Trust that there is a plan for your life and that there will be help
in living it.

At a recent gathering of healing practitioners, one man shared
a dream that he had the night before. In the dream he was in a
meeting with other healers. A woman went around the room dis-
pensing little heart- shaped pills. He noticed that there was a code

inscribed on each pill. She told him to eat the pill, and it would give him wisdom.

This dream beautifully illustrates the importance of accessing the wisdom that is in our hearts. The code inscribed on each heart-shaped pill is a clue to look to our hearts to read the hidden code of life.

It occurred to me one day that the Ark of the Covenant is a perfect metaphor for the heart center within man. According to the Bible, the Ark was a golden vessel that was carefully guarded because of the powerful force and blinding light that was emitted when it was opened.

The very creative power of God Itself is placed within soul, the Ark of God. The secret powers of soul can only be wielded by one with a pure and golden heart.

It is believed that the Ark housed the Ten Commandments that were given to Moses by God. For a moment imagine that, instead of containing God's commandments to soul, a list of "Thou shalt nots," the Ark contained God's gifts to soul: Immortality, creativity, wisdom, power, and freedom.

What if the lists of rules and commandments were actually established by religions and societal institutions to keep man ignorant of the gifts of soul? A fully empowered soul has a great deal of wisdom and spiritual freedom, and may outgrow the bounds of the institution that wants to shape and contain it.

As soul matures spiritually, it moves from obedience to an outer authority to a deep obedience to an absolute inner authority. A spiritually mature individual, through an inner alliance with the Holy Spirit, naturally embodies the qualities of fairness, integrity, and love, because he has become one with the source of all good.

Soul's power and energy come from its direct connection with the light and sound of God, the twin aspects of the Holy Spirit. This energy is stepped down through various transformers, the inner bodies and chakras, in order to make the energy available to run the body and mind. When this spiritual connection is severed, the body dies. When the connection is weak, the body and mind weaken and lose vitality.

One of the very best things we can do to revitalize the body and mind is to strengthen the connection between the human consciousness and soul through a daily spiritual practice. We must go within and bathe in this inner light and sound to remove impurities, sharpen our faculties, invigorate and inspire us. A spiritual exercise, or period of contemplation, is like the process of recharging a battery. Your life force depends on your connection to soul. Your health and happiness depend on your connection to your heart.

As an exercise, close your eyes and imagine that you are holding one of the heart-shaped pills. Notice the code embossed on the pill. The code is the key to unlock the wisdom in your heart. Place the pill in your mouth and let it dissolve. The nutrients and energy of the pill move to your heart center, and then radiate throughout your whole being. Feel your heart open to share its wisdom, love and goodness with you. You are one with the wisdom in your heart.

Take this "medicine" every day for several days, or whenever you feel tired and need a boost. As your heart heals and restores itself, you will find a renewed interest in life. Your heart can help you remember the life you were meant to live.

Chapter 7

The Secret Laws of Life

As we become more aware, we begin to discover the secret laws of life. These laws exist as a natural effect of the existence and action of Spirit in this world. They are as real and as infallible as the laws of science. They are as reliable and as unchanging today as they were during ancient times. They will work for you and on your behalf as well as they did for Moses, Jesus, or for any spiritual giant, scientist, or great artist in history. The spiritual laws are impersonal, designed to perpetuate and serve all of life. We need only to seek out the understanding and proper application of these universal laws. An understanding of the laws of life can help us heal.

We discover some of these laws through experience or through observation. For example, we often learn about karma, the law of cause and effect, by noticing certain small details of daily life. If I eat a cheese pizza at night, I might notice that I have a stuffy nose the next morning. Then I notice that the same thing happens when I eat ice cream. If this pattern continues, eventually I would put two and two together and figure out that the excess consumption of dairy products creates congestion in my body.

When we become aware enough to notice cause and effect in the small details of life, we can make the leap to the larger, spiritual implications of this law. For example, we may notice that when we complain or gossip, we feel bad. Things don't go right. Or if we are feeling depressed, we find that taking a walk, putting on some uplifting music, or doing something for someone else makes us feel better. We begin to figure out that we have some control over how we feel. When we take responsibility for our feelings and thoughts, our lives go better. We learn that an understanding of the law of cause and effect allows us to choose to be cause instead of the unconscious effect of our circumstances.

The conscious application of divine law can change your life. We normally think of principles as ideas, or ideals. But very often we see them as removed from us, and not really related to day-to-day living. Actually, a spiritual principle represents a potential, a latent energy, that can only be released through realization first, followed by an act of conscious application. Spiritual principles are the mechanisms of divine power, bringing this power to bear in our lives in specific ways.

The first law of Spirit is the one upon which all others are based. It states that all of life is Spirit. Spirit is the source of all life. This law brings us to an examination of the nature of supply. If Spirit is the source and substance of all life, then it is also the source of all supply. Our supply is not dependent on our jobs or circumstances, but is related to our level of understanding and state of acceptance. Our circumstances reflect our state of consciousness.

Divine creation might be called the eternal dream, first cause. Because we share in God's creative power, we are first cause in our own personal universe. We send out creative power through our thoughts, images, and feelings. When we have been trained instead to react to outer causes, we become the effect. We cave in upon ourselves, become introverted, and lose our connection to the source of supply.

The first step in healing our lives is to come to an understanding and acceptance of the first principle: All of life is Spirit. We are of the same substance and nature as It. We share its properties and potential for good and continual expansion.

The second universal law is that soul is the individualized essence of Spirit. Soul is eternal and is a distributing agent for Spirit. We have mastered the power of the second law when we recognize ourselves as soul and know our place in the divine order of life as an instrument of Spirit. We operate under divine grace. The universe meets us with assistance when we desire to co-create with Spirit for the good of all.

The third spiritual law in operation in this universe is the law of opposites. Everything exists in relationship to its opposite. There are mountains and valleys, age and youth, wealth and poverty. Life can be a perpetual swinging between these polarities until we learn that they exist to teach us balance. Balance is created by learning the value of the middle path, the path of not dwelling too long in any extreme. For example, periods of illness can teach us the value of health. Being temporarily broke does not mean we are poor if we know how to recreate our lives through the creative powers of soul. Experiencing the polarities of life gives soul the opportunity to test its survival abilities. Life becomes a spiritual exercise in creativity. Detachment is a part of the law of opposites. We can survive extremes when we have the emotional balance to see above the limited human view of the situation. Soul is eternal.

The fourth law is the law of vibration, or law of harmonics. Everything vibrates. Therefore everything creates a vibrational effect. Through the principle of resonance, our energy is affected by those things, people, and ideas with which we associate. An awareness of the law of harmonics helps us to consciously choose what we want to vibrationally affect us. We choose our reading material, television shows, conversations, and even our very thoughts carefully, knowing that they shape our state of being. Our state of being in turn shapes our health and our lives.

It is important to have in our lives those things, people, and ideas with which we are in harmony. Harmony is the basis of health. Harmony can be restored, our vibrations can be changed, by singing, playing music, and especially by chanting certain charged words, such as HU, OM, or some other mantra or sound that is sacred to you

The fifth spiritual law that affects our well-being is the law of attitudes. Unfortunately, most of our attitudes have been shaped unconsciously. We may have been trained to be fearful, suspicious, and mistrusting. We lost our childlike spirit of trust and adventure along the way. Retraining our attitude to one of devotion, spiritual idealism, and trust is necessary to obtain a state of spiritual knowing. We can learn to expect the best, instead of always waiting for the worst to happen. We are amazed when we find out how much our attitude shapes our destiny.

The secret of attitude is closely connected to the power of attention. Some attention must be given daily to the spiritual perspective. The spiritual perspective shapes our attitudes to be the ones that create a better life experience. "I can't wait for the rest of my life" replaces the unnamed sense of dread that accompanies our self-defeating attitudes. Control of the attention brings freedom. When we are focused on a problem or consumed with worry, it becomes difficult to move the attention. And yet a problem is seldom solved by focusing on the problem. Raising the consciousness above the problem, by taking control of the spiritual attention, removes the problem, or removes the distress it is causing us. Our attitudes are gently changed from within when we are in love with our spiritual ideal.

How do we focus on God if God is an unfathomable thing to us? One way to approach God is to focus on the "things of God," the principles and qualities which align us with It. Another way to keep the mind on God is to love and appreciate the gifts of God. I heard a man say it this way: "The only way I know to love God is to love my family. My family is a gift from God." Another woman heard this reminder from Spirit: "Life is for loving." She realized her attitude of separation and loneliness had separated her from love. She had forgotten how to love life.

The sixth law deals with the pictures that we carry in our minds. We store images and pictures constantly from the events that happen to us or around us. Many of these pictures are illusions, and do not accurately depict the spiritual nature of life. These pictures are limiting and defeating. However, these images are dead images until we focus the power of our attention on them. Images from the past spring to life and affect and control us when we dwell on them. We continually re-experience the fear, dread, or trauma associated with these old pictures. They trap us in patterns of unforgiveness, self-pity, regret, or grief and guilt.

Imagination is an image in action. Our inner speech, images, and thoughts must match the goals we want to reach. Often we are stuck and not progressing because we are spending so much time revisiting old pictures. We can revise the old pictures through the use of the imagination. We create new pictures by placing our spiritual goals and our dreams in their place. True contact with the inner spiritual forces dissolves the old images.

The proper use of the imagination depends on our ability to break old habits and patterns. When we look at something with our imaginations, we are looking at something that already exists, but that is awaiting its birth through us.

The seventh law is the law of unity, thinking from the whole. The human consciousness separates life into parts. It is unable to see life in its entirety. Looking at the parts creates ideas and feelings of separateness, difference, and discord. You and yours appear different and separate from me and mine. The realization of the law of unity restores a sense of wholeness with life. We begin to see that because we are part of a living, breathing whole, our dreams, goals, and desires must by the very nature of life be those that perpetuate the best for all.

Our highest good is achieved when we realize that the nature of life is to uplift all through the principle of growth. We have no envy, greed or feelings of competition, because we know that, through the law of unity, we are also blessed by the gifts that others receive. And we in turn become a blessing to life when we achieve our best. A blessing for one is a blessing for all under the law of unity.

In the next chapter we are going to see how these spiritual laws relate to our energy anatomy and how they can help us heal.

Chapter 8

You Are the Living Word

We do not learn a principle by reading about it in a book. We can gain a concept, a mental understanding. The realization of spiritual truth comes through the crucible of experience. We live the test, and we test the truths of life by living them. It is the experience that changes us and provides the fertile ground for our transformation.

Now it is time to look within and ask, "What are the aspects of my own consciousness that are keeping me from healing and manifesting my goals?"

The chakra system reflects our state of consciousness. We possess a complex internal communication system that enables our physical and divine natures to operate as one unit. If we are not healing or moving forward in life in the way we desire, we may need to restore proper order to one or more of these systems. The roots of our physical and inner illnesses lie within one or more of these centers.

I always felt that something very vital was missing in the discussion of chakras and our energy anatomy in the books and articles I read. I received an inner nudge to relate twelve particular spiritual principles to the chakras. I knew I was being given an important part of the healing puzzle. So I am not going to review the current theories about what chakras are, what they do or represent, but rather I would like to give you a fresh way of seeing yourself as an integrated physical and spiritual being.

Chakras are simply portals for receiving, assimilating, and transmitting information. Chakras can only accept the information that is downloaded through them, and cannot make a judgment or edit.

Some of the information comes from the outside world, and if we agree with it and accept it, it becomes a part of our reality, whether or not it is actually the truth. Other, higher forms of information, in the form of pure energy, frequencies of invisible light and inaudible sound, enter from the higher planes through the crown and are stepped down through various channels before reaching the human consciousness.

If the higher chakras are not open and functioning within us, and the subconscious is controlled by fears and reactive patterns, the spiritual knowledge is not available to us. When we are open, we experience more moments of pure intuition and spiritual clarity. If we are not open and not in tune with a higher guidance, we become a part of the group mind and accept mass postulates about every aspect of life and what we can expect from it. These mass postulates are used to control our thinking through our fears and expectations and can be used to sell everything from prescription drugs to automobiles. We need a balance in our lives of giving attention to both our outer worlds through interaction with other people and daily events and to our inner side through contemplation.

So what we are saying is that our state of consciousness determines what we believe is true, what we believe is possible, and how much we can accept, and by controlling the chakra system, directly influences our health. Chakras determine where and how our consciousness is manifested in our bodies by transmitting our thoughts, feelings, and beliefs. That is why healing and change must occur within the consciousness. Treating only the body provides only a temporary measure of relief.

In my work I have come to recognize six main chakras in the subtle body that are related to maintaining the physical body. They reflect the aspects of the human consciousness that are directly related to survival as a physical being. There are also six or more chakras above the body that correspond to our inner bodies and our existence as a spiritual being.

The point at which these two energies meet is the heart center. Thus, the heart chakra serves a critical role in merging the two parts of our makeup, the physical and spiritual. That is why there is so much emphasis on developing the open heart or golden heart in all spiritual teachings. If the heart is not open to receive God's love, the pure energy from the higher dimensions, we are left to function as half a being, driven by the longings and needs of the lower self.

In my practice I was seeing so many people with this split. They were so completely in the body consciousness that they were filled with anxieties, fears, and health worries. They exhibited no joy or inspiration. I asked Spirit to show me the energetics of what was going on. What was the solution?

I was shown an image on the inner screen of my mind that looked similar to computer graphics. I saw how the spiritual energies enter through the crown, the earth energy through the root and feet, and how they meet at the center, the heart. Here these energies are mixed and transmuted by the heart chakra, according to the state of consciousness of the receiver, into the energy that becomes his life. The Bible verse, "Keep thy heart with all diligence; for out of it are the issues of life,"(Proverbs 4:23) came to mind. What I realized was that because of past events, traumas, and fears, the heart is closed in many people or heavily guarded.

If energy ascends and meets a closed heart, it must return to a lower center to be played out there. If energy descends from a higher source and meets a closed heart, it, too, must return, and makes a person head centered. So some individuals are living below the belt (the co-dependents, addicts, emotionally needy, and fearful) and some out of their heads (the intellectuals and mind people), but most of us are a mix. I knew that any true healing must include a healing of the heart.

Another point should be clarified. A lot of emphasis is sometimes placed on the aura in energy based healing systems and metaphysical literature. The aura is simply the electromagnetic field around your body that is produced by your state of consciousness. It changes as you change. It is part of your own house and space and is your protection. Therefore no one can heal you by manipulating your aura, but they can unintentionally let in unwelcome visitors or psychic forces by making a tear while doing their cleansings or healings. As you would not open your door to a stranger, do not open your aura to just anyone who advertises healings or readings.

Now let's look at the twelve principles that are golden keys and can help us heal.

1. Appreciation	Gratitude, contentment.
2. Sincerity	Authenticity, being true to ourselves and others.
3. Unselfishness	Serving the universal good. Sacrifice and service. God-centered rather than self-centered.
4. Idealism	Seeing life from a higher viewpoint. An open heart. Removes judgment, blame, and guilt.
5. Devotion	Reverence. Using sound, the creative element, to uplift, praise and heal.
6. Personal Effort	Discipline of the imagination. Focus, choice.
7. Acceptance	Surrender. Self-mastery.
8. Benevolence	The law of Grace.
9. Transcendence	Detachment. The ability to rise above any situation to a spiritual viewpoint.
10. Being	
11. Knowing	
12. Seeing	

Now we are going to relate the seven spiritual laws and seven of the golden keys to the chakra system, and learn now to unleash the creative, healing powers of soul.

1. **Spiritual Law** --Life is Only Spirit.

   First Chakra- Survival. Represents our physical needs and in- stincts.

   Spiritual Principle—Gratitude

   Spiritual Lesson: The lesson of the first chakra and the first spiritual law is to let go of the feeling of need, to learn con- tentment. When we discover that life is only Spirit, we relax. We know that the needs in life and the tests of survival are tools to teach us inner reliance on Spirit and to allow us to develop our creative abilities. We learn that gratitude for the gifts of life opens us to receive and accept more from life. We can operate under the principle of increase rather than out of fear of lack by appreciating what we have. Sometimes it is through the expe- rience of lack that we develop gratitude.

2. **Spiritual Law**—Soul is the individual manifestation of Spirit. It is eternal and is a distributing agent of Spirit.
   Second Chakra-- Represents our relationship potential, including our relationship with ourselves and with God. Can be the seat of co-dependency, addictions, manipulation.
   Spiritual Principle—Sincerity, authenticity.
   Spiritual Lesson—The spiritual lesson of the second chakra and the second spiritual law is that we are soul and that we have a body. When we recognize ourselves as soul and know our place in the divine order as instruments of Spirit, we operate under grace. The universe meets us with assistance when we are sincere. We recognize others as soul also, and cease manipulating others. When we truly know ourselves, we drop self-deception and denial. We are honest in our dealings with others, and humble and sincere in our communications with Spirit. As our authentic needs are met through the first law, addictions and dependencies naturally fall away.

3. **Spiritual Law**--Law of Opposites
   Third Chakra—Seat of our self-image. Determines whether we are selfish or selfless, self-centered or God-centered.
   Spiritual Principle—Unselfishness.
   Spiritual Lesson—The lessons of the third spiritual law and the third chakra are balance and flow. In-breath/out-breath-inflow/outflow, learning/growing-giving/serving. Individuals stuck in the third chakra are stuck in in-breath, introversion. Other people's feelings aren't real to them. They don't succeed at their goals or heal very well because of the unlearned lessons of the first two chakras. Their self-focus binds their problems ever tighter to them. When aligned with soul, we discover a larger purpose in life. Tensions release. When we forget ourselves, we are free to enjoy life, be happy, and to be who we really are.

4. **Spiritual Law**—Law of vibrations. All of the influences upon soul and the body. Law of cause and effect.
   Fourth Chakra—Houses our ideals. Seat of love, including self-acceptance.

Spiritual Principle—Idealism.
Spiritual Lesson—The lesson of the fourth spiritual law and the fourth chakra is harmony. Harmony begins within our hearts. If we are burdened with grief, loss, regret, or bitterness, we cannot create a life of health and joy. An ideal can't thrive in an embittered, disillusioned heart. Only soul can give us the spiritual energy to move beyond our pain through an attunement with Spirit.

5. **Spiritual Law**—Law of Attitudes. Our state of being.
   Fifth Chakra—The creative power of sound.
   Spiritual Principle—Devotion.
   Spiritual Lesson—The lesson of the fifth spiritual law and the fifth chakra is discrimination. Soul longs to speak through us. It has no voice in this world unless we give it voice. The Bible speaks of the word, of sound, as the creative force. How are we spending our creative energy? Are we wasting it on complaints and arguments? What reality are we creating for ourselves and others through our speech? Are we demeaning or degrading life, or uplifting and cherishing it? The power of God has been described as the "I Am." The power of speech gives us the power to choose what part of the I Am we want to manifest, such as: "I am soul, eternal, wise, happy and free." Monitoring our speech is important. An attitude of devotion, optimism and gratitude increases our healing on every level.

6. **Spiritual Law**—The law of images.
   Sixth Chakra—The seat of our imaginative powers.
   Spiritual Principle—Personal effort, discipline.
   Spiritual Lesson—The lesson of the sixth law and the sixth chakra is the discipline of the mind and imagination. Unless the sixth chakra is operating under soul, the mind will very quickly out-create soul. The subconscious mind responds to suggestion, and the rational mind to reason. But the higher part of the mind, sometimes referred to as the higher consciousness, does not respond to reason or force. It can be approached through contemplation and invoked through the imagination. Imagination is the

seeing power of soul. The first step to creating a new life begins with an inner vision.

7. **Spiritual Law**—The law of unity.
Seventh Chakra—The point of surrender, of encountering the divine; the personal will merges with the divine will.
Spiritual Principle—Acceptance.
Spiritual Lesson—The lesson of the seventh law and the seventh chakra is wholeness, unity. When we have mastered the first six laws and have achieved harmony and balance, we have come into agreement with divine law, divine love, divine will. We are capable of serving as co-workers with God.

We are microcosmic centers, which exist as part of a larger, cohesive whole. Our lives, our circumstances, are not isolated, insignificant moments in time. Becoming aware of the larger pattern of life brings meaning to every moment.

Early this morning I was out walking with my dog, and I was thinking about the process of writing. I can only write when I hear the inner dialogue that brings the thoughts from some mysterious place within, to my conscious awareness. If I try to construct passages from my own thinking, certain points may be interesting, may even contain truth, but they are flat. They are not alive with the pulse of spiritual current. I want each word to sing. A word can only sing if it comes from that inner realm, from out of the voice of God.

Our own lives can be this way. We can plan our days and our goals, using our minds to answer the question: "What do you want?" Or we can learn to enter the quiet, inner part of ourselves where truth dwells. Eventually we can live each moment as an expression of the living word. Your life can be a song.

Chapter 9

Getting Answers –
Wrestling with God

One evening after I had presented a workshop, a woman approached me and asked about the information I had shared. She was earnestly seeking to accelerate her progress in life. Without even taking time to think, I answered: "I have passion and persistence. The rest is grace." There is no difference in human beings in the amount of power or ability that they have. The only difference is in the level of awareness of that power. And, of course, the ultimate secret is that we of ourselves have no power, except to the degree that we have aligned with grace.

I have sometimes called the unexpected blessings that come when needed my grace account. This is the spiritual account that we pay into through our spiritual passion and persistence. When we are genuinely doing our best, there are times when a miracle happens just when we appear to be at the end of our resources. At these times I think, "There must be some savings in my grace account." In other words, life gives back what we put into it.

At other times, however, the path back to grace has been a struggle. I call these times wrestling with God. This wrestling process is a deep, personal engagement with the holiness of God. It is a struggle between submission and aggression, surrender and action. It is really a struggle between the human consciousness and soul — willfulness versus willingness. Wrestling with God describes the process through which we attempt to move from confusion to contentment, from complication to certainty.

The struggle comes when we are being moved into a spiritual change more quickly than the human consciousness can adapt to it, or be ready to accept it. It always comes back to our level of acceptance — how much love can we accept; how much of the responsibility can we accept that comes with that love. I heard someone say in a workshop once that the purpose of life is to be able to eventually accept the full love of God. It is unfathomable to imagine what that full love and power would feel like, or to imagine the responsibility that would accompany it.

And that is the origin of the inner struggles that accompany an encounter with the Divine: "What is going to be asked of me?"

During one such time of change, I had become so full of questions and doubts. What would the rest of the path be like? It was too hard; it required too much; I wasn't strong enough. And it didn't look like very much fun. I was involved in a futile indulgence of the protests of the little self. Basically my question, in a somewhat angry tone, was: "Can there be no corner in me where you are not?"

During this time I was out walking one day, a barrage of questions and doubts streaming through my mind. I came to the entrance of a set of walking trails that went into the woods. There was a bench in a small clearing. I sat down on the bench, hoping to reclaim a moment of inner peace. I noticed something shiny on the ground. I dug into the sand and retrieved the object. It was an old bottle cap. Inside the cap were written these words: "Why do you ask?" God has quite a sense of humor, and even when we fall back to less mature behavior, acting like a petulant child, the answers still come.

I sensed a great deal of patience and love in that moment, the patience of the eternal. That one question brought me up short, and immediately broke the illusion under which I had been suffering. The suffering had been very real. But it was caused by my inability to see the fullness and the majesty of the divine plan. Suffering comes because we don't know enough in that moment to fully submit to the process. We are afraid we are losing control, losing ourselves. Life is becoming something so unfamiliar that momentarily we have no bearings. The inner assurance is all that we have. Then God gives us a bottle cap or some other sign that we are not forgotten, and that we are still loved and guided.

That question, "Why do you ask," is a very important one. Our initial motives determine the answers we get, or whether or not we are answered at all. We can't storm the gates of heaven; we must be invited in.

There are three parts to the process of change — the beginning when we set our goals and anticipate the change, the large, unknown middle part of transition, and the fulfillment, or realization of our goal. The first step is easy. It is fun to dream and plan, to dream a bigger dream for ourselves. But that unknown middle part that stands between us and the realization of our dream is the challenge. It is during that time that we need answers and guidance.

These are a few things I have learned about getting answers or guidance:

- Love is the key to getting answers.
- We must be willing to let go of old states of consciousness. In other words, be willing to change.
- Listening to what life is telling us and staying aware is a key to recognizing answers.
- We are each unique. Someone else's answer may not fit us.
- A grateful heart attracts even more help and blessings.
- Some answers lie in the past. We are finishing lessons begun in the past or in past lives.
- Be honest. Some of the hardships we face during change come because we are meeting parts of ourselves that we don't like. This is the purification process. Old things that we no longer need are coming up to be burned off and eliminated.
- Ask for help in a sincere way; then let go. Answers come when we are no longer thinking about the question.

In our everyday lives, we use our five senses to gather information and feedback from life — hearing, sight, touch, taste, and feeling. There are also higher senses that are connected to our higher chakras. These higher senses allow us to access divine knowledge and understanding. They can open the doors to memories of the far distant past and also reveal glimpses of the future. They also enable us to move into an elevated state of consciousness where a greater love and purpose enfold us.

These higher senses of seeing, knowing, and being, are developed through the daily spiritual practice of prayer, meditation, or contemplation. To awaken your inner senses, begin by asking your Spiritual Advisory Team for assistance. Then do your part by sitting in contemplation daily with an expectant anticipation of having your inner sight and inner hearing opened. At first you may see an inner light. It might be blue, yellow, green, or pink, or even white or gold. The light is the reflection of the atoms of God's energy, the Holy Spirit, as it moves through the various inner planes, or levels of heaven. You may also hear an inner sound, such as the sound of electrical humming, a musical instrument such as a flute or violin, or wind or ocean waves. The sound is produced by the movement of God's energy, or Spirit, through the various planes. The different vibrational levels of the different planes produce the different colors and sounds.

Actually, each physical sense has a corresponding inner counterpart. When your consciousness has moved to a higher level during contemplation, you may smell a fragrance that wasn't in the room before. Sometimes the aroma signals the arrival of a spiritual guide. The sense of feeling, or touch, is experienced as the presence of love. You may sometimes feel as if a mantle of love and comfort has suddenly been draped around you.

We are usually tested in some way before we are opened to more flow or given access to more spiritual power. One night in the dream state, a spiritual teacher asked a small group of people this question: "If you are given more energy, what will you do with it?" I closed my eyes for a moment in contemplation. I knew that the answer I gave was important. On the inner screen of my mind I saw a child's riding toy. "Be a vehicle!" I blurted out. I knew that the only reason to have more power is to use it in service to all of life. I also recognized that the size of the vehicle, a child's riding toy, represented the fact that we are still spiritual children. Our capacities are still relatively small. There is always more expansion and growth possible if we choose to develop into greater vehicles of love and service. I think the dream symbol was also a reminder to keep the trust and purity of a child.

It is easier to get answers when we are relaxed, and almost impossible to get them when we are tense. Yet we are the most tense when we are having challenges and difficulties, the very times when we need answers the most.

Not too long ago, I found myself slipping into a state of worry. My son had developed a potentially dangerous health condition, finances were strained, and several other challenges surfaced at the same time. Even though on many previous occasions I had worked through the process of seeking inner guidance, surrendering, and receiving help, I found myself tense and worried.

One night I awoke with this thought being impressed on my awareness: "You must give up need." The inner voice continued and reminded me that the way to the way to receive God's help was to give up the feeling of need and worry, and resign my cares to God. I instantly relaxed. I awoke with a renewed sense of hope and trust.

My son's situation was soon resolved, and the other problems also worked out. I felt that I was being tested to see how completely I could live my faith — living without a net. This has happened many times, and each time I go through the experience, I learn that our spiritual freedoms must be re-won each day. We can never take the state of grace for granted, but must do our part each day to tend the field of spiritual consciousness, and cherish the delicate relationship with all that is holy.

The ways that we get answers from God are as individual and as varied as we are.

One friend told me an amusing but powerful story of how the Holy Spirit spoke to her through her automobile, teaching her a valuable lesson. Mary's family owns a car and also a big, powerful truck. Mary usually drives the truck. But when bad weather comes and the roads are slick with rain or snow, she lets her husband drive the truck, and she takes the car. She is afraid that she can't manage the truck's power when the roads are bad.

On one occasion she had not driven the truck for several days because of bad weather. Finally the weather cleared, and she got in the truck to drive to work. "So," the truck said, "Where have you been?" Startled, Mary began to explain that she was afraid to drive the truck on bad days because it was so powerful. "So what you are saying," the truck continued, "is that you are giving your power away." Mary was stunned. She realized that every time a challenging situation came up in the family, she left it up to her husband to resolve it. She used her husband's presence to avoid dealing with difficult situations. She suddenly understood that by always passing the problem on to her husband, she was missing opportunities to grow and learn.

A friend sent me this story: *"I received a phone call from my sister telling me she only had a few weeks to live. While I had not held out a lot of hope for her full recovery from a cancer that spread with lightning speed, I had not expected to be sitting in my office, crying, so soon after her recent surgery. It is stressful, waiting for someone to take their last breath, wondering if you have said all that you needed to. On this day I felt awkward and useless-- I had failed.*

She asked me to accompany her daughter to a hospice facility she had picked out for her last days, should it come to that. A hospice facility, no matter how wonderful it might be, was not what I wanted for my sister. I wanted to be there with her when she passed, in her own home. I did not want to accept defeat, but defeat and victory were not mine to parcel out. So there I was, searching deeply for an answer to why this was happening. I decided to go into contemplation and ask for help. I used a technique my sister had taught me. 'God, I really don't understand, but I am trying to have faith that everything happens as it should. If this is for the best, I really need a sign from you.' I paused a moment, wondering what sign to ask for. I remembered how much joy my sister felt when cardinals came to the bird feeder. 'God, please show me three cardinals today if this is for the best. I will be assured that everything is in your hands.'

On my way to visit the hospice facility, I kept an eye out for cardinals. None were to be seen. We arrived at the location, and I was surprised to see that it was named after a well- known Catholic Cardinal from Chicago, my present hometown. We entered the building, and the coordinator showed us around. There was a picture of the Cardinal in his robes in the hallway. There were two more pictures of the Cardinal in other rooms. We went outside. The grounds were beautiful, but not a redbird in sight.

We went back to my sister's house, and I forgot about redbirds until that evening. I began to feel let down. 'I've not seen the birds. Is this my answer?' 'You asked for cardinals, and they've been shown to you directly,' an answer came from within me. I had seen three pictures of the Cardinal at the hospice facility! I felt such relief and gratitude at that moment. I was deeply aware that we are all helped and guided all of the time, but we don't always recognize it. I also understood that healing is about letting go, and that my job was to open my heart to let Spirit enter and make Its home there with love. Whatever was needed would be done, in the way that was best for all."

A healer named Diane shared with me that she had always had special help from spiritual beings from the time that she was a child. These spiritual helpers were there during some traumatic times, providing the only safety and stability that she knew. She always knew that no matter what, this inner source of help and comfort was with her. As she grew up, she continued to ask for help from her spiritual guides whenever she had decisions to make. It didn't matter how trivial or serious her question, she always got the answer she needed. She said that she had learned that her decisions in life did not have to depend on her intelligence, personal abilities, or information available to her from an outside source. The answers that she needed were there just for the asking. She said that she now recognized that from her childhood experiences, she has learned to live in the presence of God. She grew up trusting in that presence and the help that it would provide. Her experiences taught her to live in the moment, with trust and with love.

Diane has learned the secret to getting answers. She has learned that she is always on holy ground and in the presence of God, as we all are. Our task is to learn not to indulge the mental and emotional states that separate us from that presence. Nothing in the world can ever separate us from the love of God except ourselves.

Chapter 10

The Creation of Health

The phrase, creation of health, implies that healing is a creative process. Indeed it is, as is every other aspect of life. I don't know the origins of the story, but when a mountain climber was asked why he wanted to climb Mt. Everest, he replied: "Because it is there." Why do human beings feel compelled to create, to express? Because we can. The creative impulse exists at the very core of our being and is tied very directly to our happiness and well-being.

We call high forms of creativity art. When an art form fulfills its spiritual purpose, it awakens something within us, and fans our desire to be and do more.

To create is to be happy and fully alive. When we are in the midst of the creative process, we are in a close relationship with the substance of life. We are in a state of flow that brings a keen aliveness and awareness. We are transcendent.

For some, this process involves an art form, such as painting, writing, or dancing. But others have found that they experience this flow when they are playing their best game of golf, gardening, cooking, or at a time when they are simply enjoying a special sense of oneness with nature or all of life. An ordinary activity becomes a creative expression when we bring consciousness and intention to it.

Are creative people happier and healthier than other people? Generally, but only if they have learned how to transfer the secrets of the creative process to the everyday moments of life. We all know the stories of creative geniuses who became alcoholics, committed suicide, or died alone and unhappy. Having once tasted the supreme act of creation, is life worth living without it?

Our task is to learn how to contact this creative substance of life, the Holy Spirit, on a daily basis, and to live in and from Its presence. We are all artists. Life is our canvas. An act of creativity can be a peak experience, but perhaps the result or outcome isn't as important as the process itself. It is through the creative process that we learn how to be God-like. Someone may be a great musician or artist, but apart from the artistic moments, their lives may be unhappy and unfulfilled if they haven't learned to hear the secret voice of God that is speaking to them all of the time. The genie, soul, is longing to be out of the bottle, to release its powers of creativity and livingness into the world through us everyday.

Is this, then, the secret to true happiness and health?

Perhaps you are currently too ill to feel creative. If you still have the power to think, to envision, you have the power to create. Regardless of your present condition or circumstances, starting now, make a contract with yourself and God to be your best, whatever that means within the confines of your current circumstances. If you have felt hopeless in the past, know that the bruises of life only served to prepare you for this moment, a moment of meeting the divine creator within you.

The butterfly only becomes strong enough to fly by struggling out of its cocoon. The struggle builds the strength needed for flight once it is free. It earns its wings and the freedom of flight. The human body wants to be comfortable, but soul wants to be free. Some of the struggles we experience this lifetime were especially designed to help us build spiritual strength.

A friend named Janet uses her creativity to get help and guidance. In a meditative state, she poses her question to God concerning health or other issues. Then she restates the question as an affirmation with gratitude, knowing that what she asked for has already been received. For example, in asking about her job, she might ask: "Should I continue to work at this job which I dislike but for which I am well paid?" Then she restates it this way: "Holy Spirit, thank you for divine guidance and peace without reservation." Once she makes a decision, she proceeds with the information at hand, and doesn't change direction unless she receives guidance that she should.

She says that there are other times when she knows exactly what to do, even when the inner guidance seems to defy all logic. She calls these her "God times," and has learned to follow the inner instruction without fear or reservation. When she asks about her health, she may be told to take certain herbs, use specific exercises, or to simply see herself as whole and healthy. Once she sees herself as healthy, she has learned that she must not go back to picturing herself as unwell. Janet said, "It is truly amazing how much power we have to help ourselves."

What is the creative process, and how does it work? As cause in our own personal universe, we send out creative energy through our thoughts, imaginings, and feelings. But is our energy—our thoughts, feelings, and imaginings—going in the direction of our goals? Mastering the direction of our energy is the key to success. Harnessing the power of our feelings and thoughts takes us where we want to go.

I once heard a dancer interviewed on television. He said that as a young person in school, he was often daydreaming about dancing, seeing the whole choreography unfold in his imagination. This daydreaming often got him into trouble. He said that today he gets paid a lot of money to do the very thing he used to dream about.

The creative imagination is a spiritual gift. Life becomes an exercise in using creativity to solve our problems and to move forward. We learn how to look within for solutions, thus avoiding despair and hopelessness when no help is forthcoming from outside of us.

To be successful in using our imaginations to change conditions, we must first believe that the world is not solid, and that conditions respond to our thoughts and attitudes. We also cannot believe that our problems are more powerful than we are. Whatever problems we are experiencing do not define who we are; they are merely temporary conditions. Do not identify too closely with your problems, or you will not be able to change them. You are soul. Solutions always lie in being able to raise your consciousness. If your problems and illnesses have created a lot of fear in you, know that the love that comes from contact with God's light and sound will banish fear.

A creative process is not forceful, tense, and doesn't require trying too hard. This prevents results. An inner love and interest holds our attention and focuses our energy. Creativity is simply a combination of thought and feeling, a deeper level of receptivity.

The law of unity holds the potential for diversity. You, as the individual channel, provide the center for the diversification of Spirit.

Your thoughts and ideas are the seeds of potential. Your love for your ideal nourishes the seed and enables it to germinate and take hold in your consciousness. It is love and love alone that can push back boundaries and dissolve limitations. The consciousness is the channel, the gate that moves the gestating seed from the inner to its birth in the outer world of form. The individual consciousness is the center through which the latent, undistributed potential of Spirit is realized. It can move from the general to the particular only through a specialized channel—your consciousness.

Ever single day in my work as a healer, I experience the people who come to me as living systems of vibrations and frequencies, intricate networks of frequencies of light and sound. I do not see the body as solid, incapable of change. I experience it as a volatile, moving, living potential, because it is an expression of the person's consciousness, and a living picture of their life experience.

Energy responds to energy. Your body responds to your thoughts and feelings because your thoughts and feelings are the way that you harness energy and express it. Aligning your consciousness with certain spiritual principles is the way to change your life.

When we begin to apply spiritual law directly to our lives in this way, the complex layers of consciousness begin to unfold for us. The unexplored consciousness is like the book that has been on the shelf for many years, unread.

Subtle areas of resistance and unconscious patterns emerge as the pure light of divine love illuminates them. It is only when these unknown, unchallenged parts of ourselves come to the surface, that the illuminating power of divine love can dispel them. If we are too lazy or disinterested to apply divine law to our lives, the unmanifested seeds of our own greatness lie dormant. They await some future opportunity when we are ready to become the change that we desire.

Last night I had a startling dream. In the dream, there was a small chip in the front windshield of my car. Suddenly, as I was sitting in the car, the small fracture spread across the windshield in every direction. I touched the glass to see if it was stable. It moved under my touch. I knew that this was dangerous, that the glass could break under the impact of movement. Suddenly the glass shattered, and pieces flew, lodging in my face and body. At first I called out to a friend who stood nearby to call an ambulance. Then I began to pick the pieces of glass out of my skin. When I had nearly finished, I told my friend not to call the ambulance, that I had been able to remove the glass myself. I said, "Look, it probably won't even leave a scar." I had a hundred cuts and wounds, but I knew that they would heal.

After a little thought, I realized that this dream was telling me that the windshield represented my old viewpoints and perceptions of myself that are being shattered by being the instrument for this book. The act of writing about change is changing me. You cannot enter into a close engagement with the Holy Spirit and not be changed and deeply affected on all levels by it. I knew that the dream was telling me that we are our own saviors, and that our redemption comes from the shattering of our old viewpoints. The experience can be painful, but leaves no scars because of the regenerating power of divine love.

As long as there is breath, there is potential to create anew, from this moment. Close your eyes and rest for a moment without any struggle or inner tension. You don't have to think about how to be well or how to correct your problems. You only have to be present with this love that is trying to reach you and heal you. For a time, just sit or lie in stillness, knowing that you are loved.

Before reading any further, take a piece of paper and write down one or more situations or health conditions you would like to heal. Then put the paper aside, and we will return to it later.

Part Two

Taking Responsibility–
Healing Through
Self-Mastery

Chapter 11

Twelve Golden Keys of Healing

Your body, your mind, and emotions together create a very amazing and powerful instrument that is used by Soul to gain experience in this universe. An instrument must be kept in tune in order to sound its best and play in harmony with others.

The way to stay tuned to the rhythm of life is a daily spiritual practice, a simple contemplative exercise. We will examine areas in our consciousness that might need tuning, and explore exercises that have the power to help us change. One exercise can be practiced each day, or each exercise can be practiced for a week or longer. The key is to remember that the principles represent a vibration, a frequency that can bring you greater life. Think of the principles as notes or tones in the harmonic scale. Each principle is a golden bridge to a new state of consciousness. If you feel resistance to a particular exercise, or it brings out the opposite emotion or state of being, you may be experiencing a part of consciousness that is resistant to change. Skip that exercise, and return to it later.

In this section we will climb a ladder of consciousness, much as Jacob did in the Old Testament. For the chakra system actually represents your human and divine potential — your levels of heaven. Through a series of simple exercises, you can learn to raise your vibrations and experience a greater level of health, happiness, and spiritual awareness.

Golden Key Number One

Appreciation

A friend once remarked how she had noticed how much a certain individual had changed after taking the healing classes. I explained that the process of opening to serve as a channel for healing moved the individual out of the position of being in need to the position of being the source of supply for others. Wonderful things happen for all of us when we move from introversion, where we are focused on what we think we need, to having an increased outflow because we are serving life in some way.

The first chakra, often called the root chakra, develops in the first stage of life when we are infants and are dependent on others for our food, shelter, and physical and emotional well-being. We enter the world with a need to be taken care of. Perhaps these needs are adequately met, perhaps not. A real tragedy happens, however, when as adults we still feel a sense of entitlement to have all of our needs met by someone —our mates, our friends, our employers, our spiritual mentors. It means we haven't quite grown up. It also means we are dissatisfied and unhappy, never quite having enough.

The energy that balances the first chakra is gratitude, or appreciation. Energy follows attention. Whatever we focus on increases. Instead of focusing on our needs, we can take stock of what we already have in reverent appreciation.

After my Mother died, my sister asked what we should place on her headstone. Immediately a phrase came to mind: "A grateful heart lives forever." Although my Mother certainly endured a life of much physical hardship, she always had a grateful heart. Her trips to the grocery store for the last year before she was confined to the nursing home had to be done in a wheel chair. One day she remarked, "I have heard people say they hate going to the grocery store. I think it's a privilege." That remark forever changed the way I viewed grocery shopping.

There is always a way to feel more appreciation. The everyday things around us suddenly take on a new dimension and begin to appear as gifts when we become grateful.

The first key, appreciation, brings abundance in the midst of loss.

Golden Key Number One — Appreciation

Contemplation
To be grateful for the experience of life:
Begin by writing a list of things for which you are truly grateful. If times are hard, there are still universal ways in which we are all blessed. Close your eyes and look for the bounty in your life. As you express your gratitude to God, feel God's appreciation flowing into you. Sit quietly for a few minutes and receive whatever feeling or insight that comes to you.

Action
Find at least three opportunities to verbally or in writing express your appreciation to family, friends, or co-workers.

Journal
Record the results of your gratitude exercise.

Golden Key Number Two

Sincerity

Several years ago when I first began to work with the principles of consciousness, I decided to present a workshop. I chose a date and mailed out flyers. As the date approached, I still didn't have the material I needed for the workshop. I trusted Spirit to provide the right information in time. A few days before the workshop was scheduled to take place, I still didn't feel that I had the right information to present. I decided to go home at lunch and contemplate, feeling certain that a breakthrough was near. I ate a quick lunch and sat on the couch to contemplate. I began by letting my mind drift over the concept of consciousness. I began with the mineral state. My awareness then shifted to the plant kingdom. Animals drifted into my awareness. Then I began to think about the human state of consciousness and the vast range of levels, all eventually leading to awakening to the possibility of self and God-Realization.

My reverie suddenly carried me into a visionary experience beyond my mind and senses. In the vision I saw, or rather experienced, the meaning of life. My mind could not bring back a single image of what I experienced, except that the message was very simple. I knew that every atom, every cell, every molecule of life is attempting to express its reason for being, and that the secret of life is contained within the creative power. I came out of the experience with the phrase, "All I have to do is manifest God."

When we sincerely desire to express the highest in life and our motives are pure, life meets us with help and inspiration.

I have long contemplated the meaning of the phrase, "manifesting God." The quality that makes us God-like is our ability to create. We are manifesting God in our creations when we choose to align with Spirit, the voice of God, and let Its message speak through our creations. Then we each can become a light to the world.

When I was in my twenties, I had an experience with the voice of God that came out of a deep level of sincerity on my part. I had always been extremely sensitive to the suffering of others, especially children. Hearing about a severe case of child abuse in the news could leave me feeling very depressed and helpless. This was an imbalance in my emotions that needed to be corrected.

One evening, a terrible case of the death of a young child had been reported in the news. The awful details of the crime seared my consciousness with deep pain and sorrow. I went upstairs and sat on the bed in the dark and prayed one of the most sincere prayers of my life. "Please, God. What can I do to help?" I wasn't really expecting an answer, but one came. "Be the best that you can be," a quiet voice said. Instantly the pain and anguish left my heart. My heart leapt with discovery! I had a mission! The way that I could make a difference in life was to diligently apply myself to my spiritual unfoldment. In other words, the lesson even then was — manifest God in your life.

To be sincere means to be close to who you really are, to express your higher truth and your heart's desire. It means saying what you mean and meaning what you say. Sincerity is the quickest way to the heart of God. God knows our hearts and our true motives.

The second chakra, referred to as the sacral chakra because of its proximity to the sacrum, begins its development as a child grows out of infancy and is in the process of becoming aware of itself as an independent, separate human being. The child is also old enough to begin interacting with others. Concepts such as respecting the property and rights of others surface as children play and must learn the rules of getting along. The concept begins to dawn that life isn't totally about me and my needs. Others live in this world, too. This stage of consciousness provides the opportunity to learn the cardinal rule- treat others as I would like to be treated- or to learn manipulation and deceit. Get what I want at all costs. Sincerity is the principle that balances the energy of the second chakra.

To be sincere is to honor the true self. Sometimes we interpret honoring the self to mean blaming others when we feel we are not respected or treated fairly. It becomes an excuse to become petulant or defensive instead of truly sincere. Being sincere means we take time to ask, "What is the loving thing to do?" Not, "How can I protect my ego in this situation."

Many times when we want to improve an unpleasant situation in our lives, we lament that nothing seems to change no matter what we do. Yet, at the bottom of things is the truth that we are not really sincere, that we are not really honest with ourselves. We want things to be better, but not if it means we have to change. An authentic life requires that there not be discrepancies and gaps in our inner and outer lives.

Once a friend shared a dream with me, which illustrates this point. In the dream a teacher drew two parallel horizontal lines on a board, representing our inner and outer lives. The teacher said that when our outer lives align with our highest self, we begin to live the high life. What we truly think and believe must align with what we say and what we do. Living a lie is a roadmap to disaster. The amount of power we have to elicit help from a divine source is directly proportional to our level of sincerity. Sincerity means aligning ourselves with the highest, most sacred part of ourselves. The shortest path to harmony is finding the path, actions, and beliefs which align the human consciousness and will with Soul. Golden key number two, sincerity, can bring peace.

Golden Key Number Two — Sincerity

Contemplation
Close your eyes and ask God to show you how to be your true self. Sing, chant, or just silently repeat the word sincere three times. Sit quietly and listen. Soul is waiting for you.

Action
Make a list of areas in your life where you believe you are not authentic and true to yourself. What is your heart's desire for your life? How can you be a better listener?

Journal
Record any experiences, insights or plans.

Golden Key Number Three

Unselfishness

Before beginning a healing session, I always say some silent affirmation to declare myself a clear and open vehicle for Spirit. One
day I found myself changing my words to: "They are yours. I serve
them for you." A few days later Spirit refined my awareness a step
further: "I serve You through them." Now I was no longer working
for the client. I was working for God. I was serving God through
the client. If we can remember to do everything in the name of the
highest principle, it takes the personal element out of it and creates
the best possible outcome for everyone concerned. It also insures
that we act out of love and do our very best.

Unselfishness literally means beyond the self, the little self.
Some indications that we might be operating from a selfish consciousness are an indulgence in vanity, low self-esteem (which is
also a form of vanity), or the victim consciousness. Any state that
creates introversion has us staring so hard at ourselves that we can't
see the big picture. We think that all of the drama in life revolves
around us.

There is a place for self-interest. We do have to take care of
ourselves with our nutrition, exercise, enjoying our friends and
whatever blessings life has given us. A healthy self-interest is different from self-involvement. A deeply self-involved person can't
even see what blessings are already there or hear the quiet needs of
those around him because his own voice is so loud, and the constant
inner chatter gives him no peace.

An episode of the television show, "Frasier," illustrated this
principle. In the show, Frasier Crane is a psychiatrist with a radio
call-in show. Frasier has quite an ego at times, and in this episode
the city was holding a special day in a park to honor him and his
contributions to the city.

He was, of course, thrilled and had a speech and a special
wardrobe all planned. When the day arrived, everything seemed to
conspire to keep him from the celebration. Everything that could

possibly go wrong did. Finally he was on his way in a cab and would arrive just before the program would end.

At the beginning of the cab ride, Frasier was impatient to get to the ceremony. Then the cab driver began to open up and talk about his life and some deep personal concerns. When the cab arrived at the park, Frasier had to decide whether or not to jump out of the cab and enjoy at least a small bit of adulation from the remaining crowd, or to remain and listen to the driver and offer some professional help.

His higher calling won, and the show closed with Frasier still in the cab listening to the driver.

Everything must be done only for love.

Unselfishness, of course, doesn't mean austerity. We don't have to give up all of our worldly possessions to serve an ideal. It implies living a larger life, beyond the boundaries of the human self. Golden key number three is a golden bridge to the hearts of others.

Golden Key Number Three — Unselfishess

Contemplation
Service is its own reward.

Close your eyes. Breathe deeply. Sing the words Divine Love slowly and softly, or spell it (D-i-v-i-n-e L-o-v-e) three times. Silently ask, "What are you asking me to do?" "How may I serve?" Listen.

Action
Give a gift or service anonymously. Look for ways to put others first.

Journal
Record your experiences and insights.

Golden Key Number Four

Idealism

One morning I was changing TV channels to watch a few minutes of the morning news. I paused a moment on an old movie. A very serious discussion was taking place around a table in what appeared to be the boardroom of a large corporation. At the moment I paused, a character said, "We bring everything we are to the smallest act."

Those were the very thoughts I had taken into sleep with me the night before! I had been contemplating the importance of "walking the talk," of living the principles that we say we believe. I was finding myself daily being asked to choose an attitude, an action, or a belief that in turn would create my life experience for that day and affect those around me for either good or ill. Interestingly enough, the name of the movie was *Cobweb*. Indeed, it portrayed the web of karma that had created the circumstances being played out in the movie.

I realized that when we live unconsciously, we are committing spiritual thievery. Every careless complaint, criticism, or dishonest word or action robs us and those around us of valuable energy. As we grow and move closer to our spiritual ideals, we find ourselves healing old resentments, restoring relationships, and, in short, finishing old business.

An ideal is defined as a perfect model or standard, an archetype. In man the ideal resides within the heart. When you destroy the ideals of a person, a country, or an organization, you have destroyed the heart. The heart feeds life to the whole organism. Every path in life must have a heart.

One night I found myself teaching a healing class in the dream state. We were discussing frequencies in great detail. At one point I wrote the name Marilyn Monroe on the board and drew lines and waves to illustrate the frequency changes in the different sounds. Our name, in effect, becomes our energetic signature.

The movie industry changed Norma Jean Baker's name to Marilyn Monroe because they unconsciously knew that the frequency of the name matched the magnetic personality they wanted to create. The addition of bleached hair, some plastic surgery, and some voice training completed the picture. Had she kept the name Norma Jean, literally Marilyn Monroe would never have existed.

I awoke with this phrase from the class still resonating within me: "Forgiveness is the frequency that heals." Forgiveness includes self-acceptance. Perhaps little Norma Jean Baker was chosen as an example for the dream class because of her tragic life. She never got to know who she really was, and she felt such a need for love and acceptance. The insecurity, alcohol and drug use eventually led to her death.

How does forgiveness heal us? Forgiveness sets us free from the pain that binds us and ties us to the past. To forgive means to give forth. It means giving up the entitlement to feel injured or justified in holding resentment. To forgive means we can give forth love.

Forgiveness and atonement are closely related. Atonement is at-one-ment. Lifting ourselves spiritually to a higher vibratory level where only love resides takes us beyond the illusion that we have been injured. In a state of at-one-ment we desire only to give, to be — love.

A very wise young man once said to me that there is nothing to forgive if we stay in the present with everyone.

We discussed the heart center in some detail in chapter eight. The heart center is not only vital to our spiritual well-being, but to our physical health as well. Carrying old pain, resentments, anger, grief, and self-hatred in the heart for too long can over burden it and impede the flow of energy through it. Many immune disorders as well as the obvious heart and circulatory problems have their origin in the heart center.

Love expands the heart. Fear and worry close it. I had an experience that showed me the damage that fear can do to our physical and emotional well-being. I had been in a relationship for a year with a man I loved very deeply. Meeting him opened my heart to wellsprings of joy and love. As time went by, however, it became evident that, in spite of the deep love we shared, there were differences that made it improbable that we would ever share a life together. We both knew that it was time to close the relationship, yet it was so difficult.

When we finally parted, the grief and pain were almost un-
bearable. I awoke one night feeling terrible anxiety. My heart was
racing to the point that I knew I was in danger of a heart attack. I
knew I was experiencing the working out of the old karmic pattern
from the past that tied me to this man. Fortunately, I had the
presence of mind to do a spiritual exercise to bring my mind and
body under control. I used an imaginative technique for releasing
fear. As I went through the contemplative exercise, I heard my own
voice speak these words to me: "Everything is o.k. Things are as
they should be."

Immediately all of my symptoms disappeared. I felt calm and at
peace. The voice I heard was the voice of Soul, the highest part of
me that knew the bigger picture. I trusted it completely, because I
knew that my emotional body and mind that were experiencing the
loss and anxiety didn't have the highest viewpoint and didn't know
the reason or the outcome. But Soul did. I was spiritually back on
track.

This experience points out the value of a daily spiritual practice.

When an emergency or challenging time does arrive, we are
spiritually prepared to cope with it. Spiritual exercises build
spiritual muscle and strength in much the same way as physical exercise keeps our body healthy. We have inner spiritual faculties that
lie dormant within us but can be awakened with contemplation and
a sincere effort on our part. Then the voice of Soul can reach the
human consciousness and guide our lives in the best direction.

Another quality of the heart is compassion. One evening in the
dream state my spiritual teacher and I were walking together. A
person near us suddenly collapsed with a heart attack. My teacher
and I knelt over the person and administered healing. When we
were finished, a medical team arrived and prepared the person to
be transported, and administered oxygen and IV's. My teacher had
moved from my side and was now working along side the medical
team. I knew this was showing me that the Holy Spirit works with
all good people who work from love and do their best. When the
team had left, someone walked up to me and said, "Compassion
brings the presence of God."

Idealism is a golden bridge to the heart of God.

Golden Key Number Four — Idealism

Idealism is the ability to perceive life through a perfect pattern.

Contemplation

Close your eyes and place an ideal image in your imagination. For example, imagine the face of a guardian angel, teacher, or spiritual Master, or simply an image of what God is to you. Know that everything that comes to you flows through that ideal matrix, and likewise everything that issues from you flows through that matrix. Imagine how your life would be different if every thought and statement passed through this image before leaving your consciousness.

Action

Practice this for one day in your exchanges with people.

Journal

Record your thoughts and experiences.

Golden Key Number Five

Devotion

What is communication? It is the giving and receiving of information in some form, whether it is written, spoken, body language, or feeling. The root meaning of the word communicate is to commune. To commune is to be in sacred attunement. To truly commune with the sacred Itself or the sacred in another requires that we first be in communion with the sacred within us. Most of our daily communications, however, are hasty thoughts, words, and actions.

The fifth chakra corresponds to the throat center, the center of sound. Sound is the creative element. The number three is tied to the creative principle. The throat center is part of the creative triad within us. The sixth chakra, known as the third eye, envisions our goal. Our heart imbues our idea with love. The throat expresses our plans to carry it out. The activity of the throat center is not limited to just our spoken word, but includes writing, playing and performing music, or painting and sculpting, flower arranging, cooking, etc. Any action that communicates is your voice, and there is great power in it.

The sounds that issue from us can heal, uplift and restore, or destroy and tear down. If we are not living authentically, the throat center may be blocked. If we are not speaking the truth as we really know it, we may have trouble with our voices, our throats, or our necks.

Years ago a woman who was in severe pain came in to see me. A disc was blown in her neck and she was wearing a brace. I sensed her throat center was involved. I asked her what had happened, if she had experienced some recent trauma. She said that she and her spouse had a terrible argument. Their relationship was in crisis. She knew that if she spoke the full truth that the relationship would not survive. She held her feelings in. There was so much force behind her feelings that the energy had to go somewhere, so it blew out the neck. After we talked, she understood that in time she would have to face her fears about expressing her feelings to her mate, even if it meant that things would change.

The fifth golden key is devotion. Devotion means to fill the mind and heart with aspiration, love, and giving self over to the universal consciousness. A number of years ago I saw a cartoon taped to the refrigerator door in someone's home. It said, "I do not sing because I am happy. I am happy because I sing." This perfectly expresses the truth and power of the conscious use of the fifth chakra.

The other side of communication is silence and the gift of listening. The test is being fully present to hear what someone is truly saying or needing from us at that moment. With practice we can begin to hear the soul behind the words, the pain or need behind the anger, or the loneliness behind the criticism. All can be met with love. We can also practice listening to ourselves in a conscious way and examine why our expression sounded angry or critical. What are we feeling that we are not acknowledging? Are we asleep at the wheel and letting old patterns create our messages? True listening makes the other feel truly seen. Listening has the power to transform.

The highest form of listening is listening to the voice of God. Our daily spiritual practice develops our ability to be aware of the quiet inner voice, and develops our link with the light and sound of God. Our intuition becomes stronger, and we are more apt to see the synchronicities and messages that are speaking to us in our daily lives.

When we have mastered the secret of the fifth chakra, and our throat center is a center of devotion, we are no longer just saying prayers of love or gratitude, but in some mysterious way, our life has become a living prayer; our life is a love song to God. That is when we are living our best life.

Golden Key Number Five — Devotion

Contemplation
Close your eyes and sing a love song to God. Make it up as you go along. Be a child again. Then sit quietly and listen to God's song to you.

Action
For one day monitor your sounds. Don't grunt, sigh, groan or complain. Sing, laugh, hum, compliment others; express gratitude; make a joyful noise!

Journal
Record your experiences or feelings about this exercise. What have you learned about the sounds you make, or about the sounds around you?

Golden Key Number Six

Personal Effort

The sixth chakra is located between the eyebrows and is sometimes referred to as the third eye or spiritual eye. It is the organ of inner vision. When the heart, the throat, and the sixth chakra are aligned in purpose, we are capable of a high level of creation. The next step, taking action, manifests our creation on this plane. I call this process "converting the God stuff." Spirit is pure, unformed energy until it has a channel or mold through which to flow.

Soul in this world is in a very unique position. It stands as the middle- man between Spirit and matter. Actually, the spiritual purpose of each individual is to learn to be a conscious co-worker with Spirit and manifest Its presence through our lives and our creations.

The process through which this conversion of energy takes place is dependent, again, on the spiritual exercises, or daily periods of contemplation. We are creative centers. We cannot escape that. Every thought, word, and action has consequences. Our responsibility is to master our own natures so that the spiritual power can flow unimpeded through us. Without discipline, the mind and emotions can carry us down a thorny path of pain and unhappiness, and we leave a path of destruction behind us.

Because of its close connection to the brain and central nervous system, the sixth chakra represents the control center of the body consciousness. It influences all other chakras and through them, the endocrine system. This is also the element that houses our delusions, illusions, and misconceptions. Making a conscious decision to discover the truth about life and to become an aware, self-directed individual is vital to our physical and spiritual well-being. This begins with control of the imagination.

The creative imagination is a divine gift when rightly used, but can be a weapon of self-destruction if it is out of control, or under the control of one of the lower passions. It would be very difficult to master the use of this center by will power alone. It would require constant mental vigilance on our part to watch every thought and impression.

Although it does take some watchfulness on our part, a gentler way to harness the power of the mind exists in the practice of the spiritual exercises. The mind can be brought under the control of soul by strengthening the spiritual connection between the two.

An ancient, powerful practice that has long been used to discipline the mind and quiet it is the use of mantras or chants. You can use a universal sound such as OM, or you can simply recite with loving awareness a favorite prayer, or verse.

I very often use an ancient sound, which is the vibrational sum of all sounds, the sound HU (pronounced Hugh) which is sung slowly in a long, outgoing breath.

You can also ask for guidance in receiving a special word or sound that fits your vibrations at this time. Look for it in your contemplations or your dreams. It can even pop into your awareness during the day, or stand out on a page you might be reading in a book. If you receive such a special sound, keep it to yourself and use it in your own contemplations.

The imagination can be a powerful tool in helping us to improve our lives and heal our bodies. Many books have been written about the use of visualization in healing and changing life circumstances

Once I found myself inwardly viewing a series of images and impressions that I later described as Soul's scrapbook. These images seemed to be imprints on consciousness that have been stored, carrying information about our life, purpose and mission. I suddenly understood the meaning of the phrase, "A picture is worth a thousand words." Each image could carry a thousand impressions and thoughts, too deep for words, the language of Soul.

This awareness arose out of that experience: "It is never o.k. to not recognize and respect the divinity of each soul."

When I was in the third grade, there was a little boy in my class named Edward. I don't remember the name of anyone else in that class, but I have never forgotten Edward, yet we may never have even exchanged words. One day in class, I learned a deeply painful lesson by observing Edward. In my hometown, which was a mill village, almost everyone was middle to lower income, but some were truly in poverty. Edward was one of these. He was so quiet and shy, with his head usually down, and had sad blue eyes. One day the teacher walked over to Edward's desk and suddenly, without any provocation, blasted Edward: "You are going to grow up to be worthless just like your Father, standing on the street corner with a cup out!" Edward kept his head down and said nothing. He had done nothing to provoke this except to be the most vulnerable person in the class, the most defenseless, making him the target of the teacher's own self-hatred and anger. My heart broke for him, but I had not yet found my own voice, nor did I understand what had happened. But I knew his deep pain and shame.

Today, I sometimes find myself going in my imagination, on the inner, to the Edwards I have known. I embrace them with love and acceptance, seeing them as the beautiful Souls, tender and pure, that they really are and always have been.

Love, forgiveness, and mercy are not bound by the limitations of time and space.

This love and grace can also be extended to ourselves. During the time that I was dealing with the memories of the childhood abuse, I had a dream one night in which I saw myself as a baby sitting on a table. The baby was wounded and sad. I rushed over to her and grabbed her in a close hug. "I love you, baby Susan," I earnestly whispered to her. Soul can heal all parts of itself.

The gift of the sixth chakra is that it provides the tool and the ability to heal the past and create the future with all of the love, joy and compassion we have within ourselves. When complaints and questions of the mind are stilled and the emotions become quiet reflective pools, then Soul slips its images into our awareness, and our outer lives begin to reflect It.

Early in my spiritual journey I had the following dream experience. The dream teacher had a summary of my life up to that point in the form of a written composition. He had corrected the composition, much as a teacher would mark a school project. Then he wrote in large letters across a board: "And the rest of the story is...." I knew this experience was telling me that many of the karmic debts, lessons, and experiences in my life were being balanced, and that it was up to me to determine the rest of my spiritual destiny, to consciously write on the page of my own life. The sense of freedom to choose in life was exhilarating, yet I also had a keen awareness of the accompanying responsibility.

Try this as an exercise. Either on paper or in your imagination, write the words, "And the rest of the story is...." Let your heart and your imagination fill in the rest of the story.

Golden Key Number Six — Personal Effort

Personal Effort is discipline of the imagination and control of the emotions.

Contemplation

Begin by stating your desire to have your mind and will aligned with the purpose of Soul. Sing or chant a word or mantra such as HU, or recite a verse or prayer that uplifts you. Sit quietly, and then place in your mind's eye a situation or problem that you would like to view from a higher viewpoint. What is a positive outcome or solution that you can envision? Let your heart fill with love. Know that Soul is already working for your highest good when you align with It. Give thanks for the experience of the problem and the opportunities for growth it is bringing you.

Action

Make a list of things you can do to enhance your inner life. Examples: Contemplate daily. Read, journal, and record your dreams. Take solitary walks.

Journal

What awareness or feelings arose during your contemplation?

Golden Key Number Seven

Acceptance

The pace at which we can expand our consciousness is dependent on our ability to accept change. Some changes are welcome, such as receiving a pay raise, taking a vacation, falling in love, etc. We view these changes as gifts. Other changes can make us uncomfortable and even downright unhappy because so much is required of us. Although we don't recognize it in the beginning, these changes often bring the greatest gifts. In the beginning, though, we would like to return some of these gifts to sender, unopened.

Two years before my Mother's death, I had a dream that she had received a large bill that had come due. At the bottom of the paper, I read that I was responsible for paying a portion of the amount for her. I awoke with a very uneasy feeling. I knew this meant some kind of change was coming for my Mother, and something was going to be demanded of me in the process. It looked as if there might be a high price tag on this experience. I asked in contemplation to understand the meaning of this dream. What I understood was that my Mother had agreed to burn off a huge amount of karmic debt during the last portion of her life in order to be free of more of her unfinished business.

In other words, it was an agreement to grow spiritually to a higher level, even if it meant much suffering. Because of her age and her frail health, there was limited time for her to accomplish this. I had agreed to help with her process so that she could meet her spiritual goal. All of this was at the level of Soul. My Mother had no conscious recollection of this agreement, and neither did I, except for the dream.

Sure enough, soon my Mother began to experience one catastrophic illness after the other. She was already deaf, and she lost her vision. She developed a serious condition that required emergency surgery. She then developed cancer and had more surgery and radiation. Then there were broken bones. There was another surgery to reverse the original one. And finally, heart failure. All of this in a two year period in the life of an 86 year old, 90 pound woman. I began to think that neither of us would survive the ordeal. But time after time, she mustered the strength to go on. She said one day that she had begun to talk to God when she was alone and that God answered her.

We can accept the changes that life throws at us as graciously as possible, but it is also o.k. to ask for help when we have reached the limit of our endurance. My Mother's radiation treatments were taking place during the hot summer months. My car air conditioner was broken. She was weak and ill, and I was exhausted. One day as I was driving to pick her up for her treatment, I knew I was beginning to be too weak myself to be able to carry on my work and life and continue to take care of her as well. I silently asked for help to just get through the next few hours. Instantly the car air conditioner came on! I was asking for spiritual strength, but got a bonus as well. By the time I arrived at my Mother's apartment, the car was nice and cool. "When did you get the air conditioner fixed?" she asked. "Today," I smiled.

I also began experimenting with the power of sound to raise my energy during this time. I would chant and sing in the car, and found that about ten minutes of chanting a charged word or a sound with a high vibratory rate, as we discussed in other chapters, would significantly lift my energy and my spirits.

Acceptance is the principle of surrender. It corresponds to the energy of the crown chakra, and is a key to true spiritual unfoldment. It is interesting that the first chakra, need, is balanced by the harmonic of gratitude or appreciation, and the seventh is acceptance. The steps in between are steps in consciousness that prepare us to accept more of God's love, our only true need. An affirmation that I have often used in a writing exercise is: "I am accepting God's love for all of my needs."

What are some barriers to acceptance? Sometimes we do not feel worthy to have the gifts of life, and we are afraid to ask. Any kind of introversion, as we already discussed, blocks acceptance. When we are grateful for the gifts we already have and share through love and service, we are in essence spending the energy that we have and are opening to receive more.

When life and its burdens become more than we can bear, that is when it is definitely time to take stock of our blessings and find a way to be grateful, even for the hardship. Can we uncover in our hearts that we love God and life more than we love our problem?

After we have done all we can to the very best of our ability to resolve our circumstances, then we must humbly lay them down, and be willing to accept whatever outcome is ours to receive. This inner process that we each must discover for ourselves leads us through complication to humility, to gratefulness, to true surrender. Then miracles happen.

Golden Key Number Seven — Acceptance

Contemplation

Close your eyes. Chant or sing HU, God, or Love.

Ask, "What can I give?" Then, "Show me how to accept more love in my life."

Sit silently and feel God's love for you.

Action

Remember that acceptance is tied in with gratitude, so make a continued effort to be aware of life as a gift, and count your blessings. Say "Yes!" to life.

Journal

Write about what you have learned about giving and receiving.

Golden Key Number Eight

Benevolence

One morning I awoke with this phrase resting lightly in my awareness: "Love is our natural state." Many days I awaken in this wonderland of love. On these days God's music and love resonate within me in a greater, more blissful way, a constant reminder of the Presence, and the love and purpose of life. I find myself in love with the mystery of my own life, for it is the wonder and awe of this inner, secret side of life that has kept me moving forward all of these years.

The discovery of truth is a deeply personal process for each individual. When I heard the words, "Be the best that you can be," I knew I had just been given my spiritual goal for my life, phrased in a way that I could accept and understand at that time. What I didn't know then was that living your best life doesn't necessarily mean living the easiest life, or even the happiest life, by world standards. But it is the most honest life, the one in which we are willing "to go through it in order to get to it." (This is the phrase a friend of mine used to describe the spiritual life.)

I read this story that rang true about the called life. A reporter was interviewing a community of monks. He asked each of the monks if they were happy with what they were doing. Some said that they were happy. One said that it was difficult but rewarding. Another one said that what they were doing there had nothing to do with happiness or unhappiness. They were simply following the call of their souls. He said the question was irrelevant.

Benevolence implies that there exists a greater state of love and grace that is available to us. The state of grace does not leave us, but rather we move ourselves very far away from it and our natural state of love when we lose the connection to Soul. True healing is a return to love. I found a note I had written in the back of one of my books expressing a realization I had: "The love we withhold is the pain we carry with us."

One day I had an appointment at an animal hospital for my puppy. As we sat in the waiting room waiting for our appointment, I could see into a treatment room where the doctor who was the original owner of the hospital was working. He had sold the practice to a younger doctor and only worked three days a week. The doctor was working with an aging cat whose health was deteriorating. The cat's owner, an older woman, stood by anxiously. I assumed she and the cat had been companions for many years. As the doctor spoke to her about the cat's health, she began to cry. The doctor put his arm around her and spoke softly to her. At that moment he became healer to both the owner and the cat. He had great skill gained over many years of experience, but he also had love.

Recently the movie about Charles Lindbergh's flight, *The Spirit of St. Louis*, was on television. I watched a few minutes of it. A large crowd had gathered to witness this historic takeoff. As he and a technician were readying the plane for takeoff, he realized he needed a small mirror to attach inside the plane to assist in reading gauges. He asked the crowd if anyone had a small mirror. A woman stepped forward and handed him a round mirror from her purse. He asked her where she was from. She had traveled a long distance to be there. He asked why she would travel so far just to be there. "Because you needed the mirror," she replied. No event, great or small, unfolds in a vacuum. It takes the cumulative steps and contributions of many, large and small, each essential and timely.

Many times others have provided gifts or services needed just as I was reaching a turning point in my own life and work. The principle of benevolence, the Law of Grace, has been an ever present reminder in my life that I am not alone, and that I am loved and supported every time I am doing my very best with love. We reach the heights of God not alone, but with the love and goodwill of those around us. Withholding love or withholding our gifts and talents from life interrupt natural flow. Love is the current that carries our projects, our dreams, and our lives forward.

We can learn to say yes to life. To practice, stand up and extend your arms out to the side, as far as you can reach. Take a deep breath. To have the chest and heart so open and exposed may feel uncomfortable at first. Affirm that you are saying an unconditional yes to life. Even when we feel fearful, we can approach life with acceptance, trust, and benevolence.

Golden Key Number Eight — Benevolence

Contemplation

Is there anyone, past or present, from whom I am withholding love? Am I angry, resentful, or unforgiving toward anyone? To experience the principle of benevolence in our lives, we must extend this same principle to others. See yourself inside a cave with a brightly burning fire. This is the holy fire of purification. It can burn and purge old burdens from your heart. Sit close to the fire and feel the heat on your body. Your chest becomes hotter as the old injuries are removed from it. When the burning is complete, step outside and take a cool drink of water from a nearby cup. Repeat this exercise as often as needed.

Action

Practice being kinder to yourself and others. (This includes not speaking harshly about yourself or others.)

Journal

Write down examples of how God's love and the love of others have helped you.

What are you learning about giving and accepting love?

Golden Key Number Nine

Transcendence

There is a raw beauty and strength in the human spirit that touches me — the willingness to go through hardship if it means growth, to be uncomfortable at times if we can create, to give up attachments if we can be free. Life is full of stories of courage, strength, and survival.

Transcendence is the principle that enables us to survive in a state of peace and purpose, even in the presence of great distress. This implies that, in spirit, we are able to access a higher state of being that carries us above our difficulties so that they do not crush us.

Transcendence is related to detachment. If we are deeply attached to a particular outcome in a situation, we cannot rise above it to a greater viewpoint. If our emotions and minds are consumed with the problem, the problem is running us, and we have a poor chance of resolving it. Spiritual detachment doesn't mean that we don't care. We care deeply. It means that if something is taken from us, we feel the normal emotions of grief and loss, but the loss does not destroy us. We are able to return to balance and a loving and giving life, humbler and wiser, perhaps, rather than hardened and embittered.

A very dear friend of mine went through a major turning point when he was in his late fifties. He lost his job and then became very seriously ill. He had meditated for years, but now an examination of his spiritual life became even more important to him. One day while in meditation, he saw a tumultuous storm. A voice said, "Come into the boat, for I am the boat. But I am also the storm." This story represents the two faces of the Holy Spirit that we encounter in our spiritual journey. Spirit is the comforter, but it is also the wind of change that tears everything from us, if necessary, to bring us to a more authentic relationship with It.

I know there have been times after recovering from an illness that I have felt lighter, as if something old had been removed from me. As the events of life add to the weight we already carry, our spirits lose their lightness and joy, and purification must come in some form. We must be light to rise toward God.

Some people seem to have a natural ability, probably earned in a previous lifetime, to live in a transcendent state. For most of us, however, it takes years of living the ups and downs of the human consciousness before we seek a way to find a higher road. Spiritual equilibrium is not something that we obtain in a flash and it stays with us forever. It must be re-won everyday as the trials of daily life test us. Nor is it always a steady upward climb. Each of us carves our own individual path out of the raw material of life, and we alone are responsible for the route we take.

I am grateful for every experience I've had, even the ones that look like mistakes. The lessons that are learned the hard way tend to stick with us, as they burn an impression into our consciousness. But I was even more grateful when I learned the easy way, which consists of a daily spiritual practice to open my awareness to the light and sound of God. Life then became a joy and an adventure beyond anything I could ever have imagined.

Golden Key Number Nine — Transcendence

Contemplation
Close your eyes and sit quietly a few moments. Think of someone or something that opens your heart and fills it with love. Then picture yourself on a grassy hilltop. You are holding a large group of colorful balloons. They begin to lift you, and you float upward easily, joyously. Your heart feels light and happy as you rise. Let your journey take you where it will. When complete, gently float back down to your hilltop.

Action
Practice being conscious today. Choose to be happy and peaceful in all circumstances.

Journal
Write about any situation that is bothering you, or jot down a goal or dream. Then in your imagination, place the paper in a basket tied to your balloons. Let it float away.

Golden Keys Numbers Ten, Eleven and Twelve

Being, Knowing and Seeing

Being, knowing, and seeing are qualities of Soul. Soul is our true identity. Soul is an individual manifestation of Divine Spirit. It has free will, creativity, and immortality.

Soul experiences life in the lower worlds by taking on bodies. The physical body provides the vehicle to gain the experience needed in order to become a more mature and conscious co-creator with life. Soul must experience life in order to realize itself.

A veil of unconsciousness is dropped over our awareness when we enter physical life, and the long, laborious process of remembering who we truly are and why we are here begins. Once while doing a healing session for a client, I heard the following phrase: "Cleansing cavities of untruth." The process of living deposits false accumulations within us. The light of Soul is dim within the human consciousness, and we struggle to remember our divine origins. Soul is a powerful, strong and happy being, but the human consciousness sees itself as the victim of life, having little power to change things.

One day, inside myself, I heard this phrase: "Truth begins where knowledge ends." Knowledge is a product of the mind. Truth is the birthright of Soul. Soul knows; mind thinks; the body senses. A friend shared the following story of an experience with the knowingness of Soul.

Kathy had been a single Mom for a while. She had begun to date her son's soccer coach. It seemed like a good match, and the relationship was moving along well. Still her mind had doubts. "Is this the right man for me?" she wondered. One day she was having lunch with her beloved, and she was silently asking for a way to know if this was indeed the right man. Her partner suddenly said, "Soul knows." He then said, "Why did I say that?" She laughed and said, "I know why." The knowing part of Steve answered her unspoken question.

A friend shared a dream that shows how Soul sees. She said that she was watching a bird, and its head began to rotate in a complete circle. I said, "That is the viewpoint of Soul! It has a 360 degree viewpoint." The human consciousness can only focus on one thing at a time, but Soul has the advantage of seeing from every viewpoint. We shouldn't make important decisions without first consulting the highest viewpoint, the spiritual view of Soul.

Soul is eternal and always exists in the present. The human consciousness, living in the world of matter, space and time, has difficulty dwelling in the present moment. Memories of the past and concerns of the future occupy much of our attention. When our attention is fully present, we are exhibiting one of the qualities of Soul.

In a recent dream a man asked me for a small serving of dip or sauce. I left the room to get the small cup of sauce for him. When I entered the next room, I saw that it was filled with tables of every kind of food imaginable, beautifully prepared and displayed. It looked so appetizing! I couldn't in good conscience give this man only a small serving of sauce when this rich bounty was available. So I took a plate and put a sampling of different items on it, careful not to load it with too much, since he had asked for such a small amount. When I awoke, I knew that this represented so many of us in our lives. We approach life with a small cup, not knowing that the riches of Soul's bounty are just a room away. When we expand our consciousness, we enter a larger room in the house of God, and are able to partake of life's spiritual riches and then share them with others.

Golden Keys Numbers Ten, Eleven and Twelve — Being, Knowing and Seeing

Contemplation

Slowly and thoughtfully go through all twelve golden keys using the phrase, "I am..."

For example, "I am appreciation. I am sincerity." And so on.

Notice how different areas in your body and awareness light up with each statement.

Action

As an exercise, start your day with the following statement: "I am Soul, eternal, wise and happy." Repeat it during the day whenever a negative thought or situation arises. Watch how it lifts your awareness to a higher state.

Journal

Take out the paper, which has the list of situations, or health conditions you wish to heal. What new insights do you have about your circumstances? Do you have any new ideas for solutions, or has your relationship to the situation changed? What is the situation teaching you?

We have a choice in life. Remember that life consists of states of consciousness. We can exist at the level of the human consciousness with its fears, problems, limitations and transient joys, or we can awaken the spiritual centers within us and bridge the physical and spiritual worlds.

The first six golden keys represent our efforts to achieve self-mastery. They represent actions we can take to spiritualize our consciousness and change our lives for the better. They link the human consciousness to yet higher spiritual centers and frequencies that can transform us. As we put the higher principles to work in our lives, our vibrations change, and our lives change.

The last six golden keys represent a higher spiritual state that we become over time when we keep up our daily spiritual practice. At this point the six golden keys of self-mastery require no thought. They are automatic because they are part of who we are. We are then moving from self-mastery toward spiritual mastery. These higher golden keys make us God-like and enable us to be conscious co-creators with the Holy Spirit. The higher things of God are then manifested through our lives.

Human Consciousness	Six Golden Principles of Self-Mastery	Golden Keys of Soul
First Chakra—Need, fear of lack	Appreciation	Acceptance
Second Chakra—Manipulation, control, addictions	Sincerity	Benevolence
Third Chakra—Self-centered, victim consciousness	Unselfishness	Transcendence
Fourth Chakra—Resentments, blame, judgment	Idealism	Being
Fifth Chakra—Complaining, criticizing, arguing	Devotion	Knowing
Sixth Chakra—Wrong thinking, delusions, illusions	Personal Effort	Seeing

Each of the higher chakras, or spiritual centers, correlates to one of the six main body chakras and operates through them when we are spiritually balanced. For example:

First—I am grateful for the gift of life.

Seventh—My gratitude opens me to receive and accept more of God's love and the gifts of life.

Second—I am sincere and honest with myself and others.

Eighth—Divine assistance is mine when I am sincere in all of my efforts and do my best.

Third—I am unselfish and share my gifts with others.

Ninth— My attention is taken off of myself when I serve others. I transcend my own problems when I serve the greater good.

Fourth—I know there is a perfect pattern underlying all of life. There is a greater purpose in all things.

Tenth—Because I see the higher view of life, I am able to exist in the present, with no regrets for the past or fear of the future.

Fifth—I choose my words and sounds carefully, for they create my world and my life and affect those around me.

Eleventh—Soul gives me the truth through intuition and knowing so that I can share it through my voice.

Sixth—I envision and expect the best and see the best in others.

Twelfth---I see truth because my mind is aligned with Soul.

With even a small, sincere effort on our part, we are met with such love, help and guidance. We should now begin to realize that the keys to heaven are within us, and only await our recognition and conscious use. But read on. There is one more vitally important key.

I heard a minister relate the following story. A famous theologian was scheduled to appear at a conference. Everyone anxiously awaited his arrival. When he entered the room, someone asked him, "What is the single most important theological principle that you can share with us?" Everyone expectantly awaited his reply. The theologian was quiet for a moment and then said: "Jesus loves me. This I know, for the Bible tells me so."

I love this story for its profound simplicity. No matter which religious or spiritual path we follow, this is a universal truth: Soul exists because God loves it. This is the golden key upon which all others are based.

Part Three

Accepting the Gift–
Healing Through Divine Love

Chapter 12

The Physics of Healing

We discussed acceptance, or receptivity, as the principle which relates to the crown chakra. When we accept something or are open to receiving it, we have come into agreement with it. In physics this is called a sympathetic vibratory response. Everything vibrates. The vibrations of one thing influence the vibrations of another through the principle of resonance. Through my healing work, I have come to recognize vibrations as the key, not only to our health, but also to our happiness and well being on every level.

As humans we are used to thinking of sympathy as an emotional response to someone's suffering. But in fact a sympathetic, or matching, vibratory response occurs on all levels of our being whenever we come into agreement with something. Our vibrations, through this sympathetic response, begin to match that with which we are in sympathy, or agreement. Unfortunately for us, most of this process is at an unconscious level. That is why awakening the consciousness is so vital to healing. If you don't know what is vibrationally affecting you through your unconscious agreements, how can you begin to change your state of being?

A familiar example of how this works begins in childhood. If a parent continually tells a child it is stupid, ugly, worthless, fat, etc., the child, under the influence of the stronger, older, authority figure, comes into agreement with these statements and accepts them as truth. At an early age, his consciousness vibrates to the frequency of unworthiness. It becomes who he is. In order for this vibratory pattern to be changed, the consciousness of the individual must change. No matter how many self-help books he reads or how many people tell him that he is wonderful, he doesn't believe it at the core of his being.

A child is also influenced by his religious and educational training. The adult or institution is, in effect, God-like to the child, representing the source of all power, control, and information.

As adults this vibrational control is wielded by the media as we are continually told through ads, movies and television shows the standards by which we should judge ourselves. We also carry unconscious agreements from past lives, which can be even more difficult to uncover and resolve. So what is the solution? How do we regain control of our lives?

Anyone who is a sincere seeker of truth will eventually stumble onto this answer for himself as I have: We can eradicate the influence of unconscious agreements by simply replacing them with a higher agreement.

This is the true meaning of the Bible verse that states that if we seek God first, all else will be added unto us. Once in contemplation I heard it expressed this way: "Love God with all of your heart, and every rightful need will be taken care of." But what are the mechanics of love? What does it mean to "love God with all of your heart?" These are the secrets we need to learn.

Our attention is the secret to managing our lives. Our attention is like a laser beam that carries the essence of our vibrations. Wherever we place our attention we are placing the core of our being and our power.   The conscious placement of our attention gives us the power to choose our vibratory state. The information and exercises in the previous chapters are designed to help us do exactly that.

There are two voices that compete for our attention, the inner voice of our subconscious that carries our unconscious agreements and programming, and the outer voice of the world. These two voices shape our lives and our whole state of being unless we make a conscious choice to return the power of our existence to Soul. Then the inner voice we listen to imbues our lives with truth, wisdom, and love.

A daily spiritual practice of contemplation retrains our attention and gradually raises our vibrations. We come into agreement with the voice of God, the Holy Spirit, which can be heard as inner sound and seen as light. Only then do we begin to truly understand the principle of acceptance, which is surrender. Thy will, not mine, be done.

Through this daily discipline we become more receptive to higher spiritual vibrations, those that carry all of the positive, life-giving qualities we desire. Old messages and agreements are replaced with this higher truth: I am Soul, and I exist because God loves me.

Chapter 13

The Love That You Are

You are loved, and you are love. The law of love encompasses and supersedes all other laws of life. What is love? Is it a feeling, an action and demonstration, or a state of being? Perhaps it is all of this and more.

There are levels of love. On the mental level, love exists as a thought of affection or goodwill. On the emotional level it is a feeling, and on the physical level it is an act or demonstration of affection, caring, or kindness. Divine love, the spiritual level of love, is unconditional, impersonal, and universal. It is a state of being that encompasses all other levels, and it springs from our contact with soul.

Love is soul's true nature. One morning I awoke with this phrase in my awareness: "Love is our natural state." But love seldom acts, feels, or behaves the way we expect it to. The higher purpose of love isn't to make us more comfortable. Its purpose is to transform us. We are unfolding centers of love.

Hate is not the antithesis of love — fear is. Fear breeds a whole host of negative reactions that erode our humanity and destroy our hope. Traits such as anger, hatred, jealousy, deceit, greed, and criticism are all children of fear. Fear has many faces, and it hides underneath our most volatile emotions. Fear blocks the creative imagination and certainly impedes the ability to heal.

If you want to know what fear looks like, imagine an icy lake during the frigid winter. The water lacks movement and flow. It is frozen in place until spring comes to thaw the ice. During an energy healing session, if the person receiving the treatment has been under a lot of stress and emotional strain, their energy is very cold. As the energy gates open within the body, I actually feel cold winds blowing through the various channels and out of the energy gates as the body releases the stores of stress and fear. Fear literally freezes our energy, stops the flow of life and movement within us. We feel paralyzed and unable to move forward. Joints and parts of our bodies may freeze up, and circulation slows down. We may be tired and listless and feel cold.

People say, "Yes, I have a lot of stress, but I handle it." Their energy tells a different story. Just because we are able to store it doesn't mean we are handling it.

What are we afraid of? How have we become so far removed from our natural state of love? Our energy anatomy, with the seven major energy centers, can be controlled by our fears, or resonate with love.

We can carry many fears within us at an unconscious level and not be aware of how they are controlling our behavior and affecting our health. Let's look at seven stages of fear and how these specific fears are reflected in each of the seven major chakras:

First Chakra — We are afraid that we will not have enough, that there is not enough to go around.
(Endocrine system affected - adrenals.)

Second Chakra — We are afraid that we are not enough, that we are inadequate, inferior, damaged.
(Endocrine system affected -reproductive.)

Third Chakra — We are afraid that we will not be accepted. The fears of the third chakra are extensions of the first two. If we are afraid that we will not be taken care of, and that we are inferior or damaged, then we become focused on ourselves to the extreme. Our fears may manifest as jealousy, low self-esteem, or arrogance and self-centeredness.
(Endocrine gland- pancreas.)

Fourth Chakra — We are afraid that we will be hurt. We build walls and guard our hearts to keep out pain. But walls also keep out love.
(Endocrine gland - Thymus)

Fifth Chakra — We are afraid that that we will not be heard. We may talk too much or very little or talk negatively. (Endocrine gland - Thyroid)

Sixth Chakra—We are afraid that we will not be seen. Our fears also distort how we see things and interpret reality. (Endocrine gland - Pineal)

Seventh Chakra — We are afraid that we are alone. If fear controls the lower six chakras, then the seventh is not open and functioning properly. We have difficulty accepting love and are not open to change. We cannot get in touch with our spiritual purpose and see the wholeness and unity of life. We lack inspiration and the true joy founded in spiritual reality. We can't "get our act together," because we are literally separated into parts. (Endocrine gland - Pituitary)

Now let's look at how an application of the spiritual principles, the twelve golden keys of healing, and the seven spiritual laws transform our fears into love.

First Chakra —The principle of appreciation makes us grateful for all that we have. The first spiritual law reminds us that everything is Spirit and that God is our source.

Second Chakra —The second spiritual law reminds us that our true identity is soul, and that all souls are equal. The second spiritual principle reminds us to approach God and others with sincerity. We discover the authentic self when we experience ourselves as soul.

Third Chakra —The principle of unselfishness teaches us that when we focus outside of ourselves and give service to life in some way, we are happier and build genuine self-esteem. The third spiritual law teaches balance between giving and receiving.

Fourth chakra —The fourth principle reminds us to nurture our ideals. The fourth law reminds us of the power of love and harmony. Fears of being hurt are replaced with trust. We choose relationships that are in harmony with our ideals.

Fifth Chakra —The fifth principle reminds us that sound creates, and that the voice is to be used to heal and uplift others. The fifth spiritual law teaches us to use discrimination in the words we speak.

Sixth Chakra —The sixth principle, discipline of the mind and imagination, reminds us to monitor our thoughts. The sixth law reminds us not to dwell on the past or worry about the future, but to use the seeing power of soul to envision our goals and dreams.

Seventh Chakra —The principle of acceptance opens us to change and growth and an expansion of consciousness. The law of unity reminds us that we are part of a divine whole, that we are connected to all of life.

It is only when we eliminate fear that we begin to discover the love that we are. When the seven levels of fear are identified and their origins located in the body/mind, they can be eliminated. Then the seven stages of consciousness become the seven levels of love:

First —I have enough. I am accepting God's love for all of my needs.

Second —I am enough. I am soul, a spark of God.

Third —I see and respect the divinity in all others.

Fourth —I feel only love.

Fifth —I express only love.

Sixth —I see only love.

Seventh —I accept love unconditionally and surrender to it. I am love.

A dear friend sent me this contemplation that came to her one day. It is a way to infuse all of the senses with love.

> *"I surrender to love.*
> *Therefore I think from love,*
> *I see from love,*
> *I listen from love,*
> *I speak from love,*
> *I feel from love,*
> *I touch from love.*
> *Therefore, I am love."*

If we can determine what is causing us to feel afraid, to isolate the fear that lies underneath our defensiveness, anger, or other emotional reactions, then we can shine the light of awareness on the source of the fear. Awareness is the first step to replacing fear with love. You can invite Spirit to show you the source of your fears in a dream. Some of our very deep fears originate in other lifetimes. Once the old image floats to the surface, it is released, and our consciousness is more fully able to operate in present time. A secret to managing fear is to be fully present in this moment.

During one time of transition in my work as a healer, I suddenly began to feel afraid. I would wake up at night, an unknown terror gripping me. During that time, I watched a movie about Joan of Arc one evening on television. I felt drawn to watch it closely in every detail. The next morning when I tried to get out of bed, I was unable to walk. It felt as if every muscle in my legs had been torn. Suddenly a scene from the distant past flashed in my awareness, a scene of being tortured on the rack, the muscles of my back and legs severed. The movie set in that time period had helped to trigger the past life memory. There were other stages of releasing this fear from this past life that I had to experience before I could move forward. This explained to me why I had always felt ill and deeply disturbed whenever anything about the inquisition appeared in a television program or movie. My subconscious mind was warning me that it was too dangerous to serve as a healer. To move forward in present time, all parts of ourselves have to be present and in agreement. It took several months for me to agree to all of the steps that followed.

The definition of change is to exchange something for something else, to replace something. In music, change is modulation, a shift of key. When we change, we are changing vibrations. We are giving up old states of consciousness so that we can shift to a higher key and vibrate more perfectly and harmoniously with the voice of God.

Your heart center can be a radiating center of love that nourishes, warms, and inspires others. As a contemplation exercise, imagine your heart center as a warm, sun-like center that is radiating warmth and light throughout your whole body. The radiance then begins to spread outside of you, reaching out into the universe. The love and warmth radiating from you is an attracting power that draws more love to you in return.

As our fears release, we begin to heal. Fear and love cannot co-exist.

Love is not divisible, cannot be separated into parts. We either love, or we do not love. If we love God, we love all parts of God. Everything in life is teaching us something about love, the love that we are.

Chapter 14

Entering the Eye of God

As an unfolding center of love, you have the power to create change in a positive way, not only in your own life, but also in life around you. This change is not directed or imposed by you, but is the result of the intelligence and discrimination of Spirit as it works through you as an instrument of love.

We must not apply the laws of change to anyone else. To do so is a violation of their individual spiritual rights. Even to pray for someone else without their permission is an intrusion into their space. To avoid taking on unnecessary karmic burdens, we can let others ask for help in their own way and in their own time. If we feel we must do something, we can say, "Thy will be done," or "May your love bless them in the way that is best for them." We can only help and change ourselves. But as we become centers of love, the best that we can be, we uplift and heal others by our presence, and by the act of giving them the space to grow and be.

While working on this chapter, I awoke one morning with this phrase in my awareness: "If you do not clearly state what you want to do, you will become an effect." In Chapter 5, I said that you might find yourself being asked, "What do you want?" If you haven't yet had that question posed to you on the inner, consider it now. But first, I will share with you my experience with that question, and how it changed my life.

During contemplation, I found myself transported to this scene in an inner world: I was walking on a path that led to an ancient monastery. As I approached the monastery, I saw that the spiritual master who is the abbot of the monastery was awaiting my arrival. He was dressed in a white robe and had long white hair and a white beard. When I stood before him, he said only four words: "What do you want?" I thought for the briefest moment, the choices flashing quickly through my mind. Then I knew there was only one answer that I could give. "I want to help. I want to do God's work." "Then enter the Eye of God," he said. As he spoke these words, a huge vortex of energy appeared at his side. Without having time to think, I was instantly inside the swirling mass of energy. I could feel no separation between myself and the atoms swirling around and through me. I was of the same substance, one with it. Then the experience was over, and I found myself back in my chair, back to full awareness of my physical surroundings.

I didn't know why the experience happened, or what the implications of it would be. I knew I had been there by invitation, not by chance. I didn't know in that moment that entering the Eye of God is like entering the eye of a storm. A storm of that magnitude clears a huge path, totally changing the terrain over which it passes. My answer gave the Holy Spirit permission to begin the necessary changes that would prepare me to serve as a better co-worker with God. Years later, I jokingly told some of my friends that the next time I sign a contract with God, I would read the small print.

If the genie gives you three wishes, are you going to waste them on sausages, as the couple did in one fairy tale? Why not go for the gold, the highest spiritual goals you can imagine, such as self and God-realization? Then the smaller steps and goals take shape for us in manageable portions, so that we do not become imbalanced or change too rapidly. When we seek the spiritual consciousness, we are choosing the gift that never stops giving, the gift out of which all others spring.

If you are bored and your life lacks challenge, your goals are too small. Maybe you are afraid to expect too much, or feel that you are not worthy or gifted. Remember that all souls are equal, and that divine grace is not limited in the way that it can bless us.

One day a friend left me a great message on my answering machine. She had gone to the grocery store, and the clerk at the register was a petite woman with the most joyous disposition. My friend looked at the woman's nametag. It said, "Enormous." My friend asked, "Is Enormous really your name? What is your last name?" The woman answered, "Little." Her name was Enormous Little. My friend thought about the significance of this experience. In the human consciousness we are small, but the powers of soul are enormous. As human beings, we embody the great within the small.

The love that we are can reverberate throughout the universe, just as dropping a pebble in the water sends ripples in ever-widening circles.

When we enter the Eye of God, we develop a singleness of focus and purpose that marshals all of our forces in one direction, so that no energy is wasted. Every event, great or small, has meaning, and moves us steadily toward our goal. Being in the Eye of God also means that, though the world may shake and quake around us, we exist centered in love, calm in purpose.

When we withhold love, we are keeping the fullness of God's love from reaching us. If we separate ourselves from one, we separate ourselves from the whole. If we wonder why we feel isolated and unhappy, we need look no further than our own feelings and actions. God or life isn't punishing us, but certain centers within us are closed because of our pain, unhappiness, and fears, and are preventing the ever-present help from reaching us.

It is a difficult thing to do, to be enormous rather than little, and we choose between the two everyday. We strive to not waste time on guilt or remorse over the times we are less than we desire to be. We recognize that we have done the best we can, and others have done the best they can, also. As we grow in awareness and know more, we do more.

There are so many events in my own life, so many times that I know I simply didn't have the capacity to love enough, and I made mistakes. But the experiences of life teach us humility through our suffering, and we learn to turn to a greater source of wisdom and love for answers. And slowly our capacity to be love grows. There is always another step in life, because Spirit is the principle of increase.

One night in a dream I was watching a family interact with each other. They were loud, poking fun, and sometimes openly criticizing each other. I looked at this scene and thought, "This is love, too." In the expanded awareness that I had in the dream state, I could see the love they had for each other that lay underneath the imperfect behavior. They didn't know how to show or express it, but in their own way, they were learning how to, and how not to love.

And that is what life is teaching us all. An invitation to heal is the invitation to open to greater awareness of the love that we are and always have been, but have been removed from it through the process of living. We exist because of that love, and the gift of life exists because of that love.

So what is healing? I have come to believe it is the coming into a fuller awareness of ourselves as soul. Along the way, many old wounds and hurts disappear. The body will always have repairs to make and germs to fight off, so we don't want to focus all of our attention on healing the body only. No healing of the body is ever permanent, but an ever-expanding awareness of your spiritual heritage and potential is yours forever. There are many routes to the divine because of the uniqueness of soul. Even within a religion or spiritual teaching, each individual will seek and experience truth in his own way. We each are a path and a way.

If we love life and are able to see the gift in all things, even the hard times, we have learned the secret of healing. Problems come and go, and always will, but they matter little when we know that this love that we are carries us ever deeper into the heart of life, into the Eye of God.

Conclusion

A book about healing should, in the end, offer hope that things can and will be better. We have discussed seven stages of healing that relate to the seven major energy centers of our bodies. The energy centers, or chakras, reflect and represent aspects of our consciousness. They can do no more for us than our present state of consciousness allows. So healing involves some level of responsibility, awareness, and self-mastery. Healing involves change.

Healing ourselves is the hardest work we ever do. It is Soul's work. It requires authenticity and sincerity. It requires keeping an open heart in the midst of our pain. It also requires us to delve into the secret chambers of the self to uncover Soul's agreements with life. What have I agreed to learn, to do, to be?

Hopefully, by breaking the process down into these stages and steps, you have been able to identify some things that you can do to enhance your well-being. The seven stages of healing represent aspects of our consciousness that may be out of spiritual alignment. Misalignment blocks the healing power of love.

The process of healing is about uncovering the unconscious motives that drive us, the blocks that bind us, the patterns that enslave us. True healing leads to freedom. What good is it if we relieve a pain, but our hearts remain empty?

The heart must be open before we can give love, and the crown must be open before we can receive love. This level of giving and receiving divine love is different from the distorted versions of love experienced through the first three chakras. Without the intermingling of the spiritual forces, our expressions of love are based on the needs, longings, and fears of the human consciousness. A gift given at this level always expects a return, and love is often wielded as a weapon of control. Lust and greed breed further corruptions that are very far removed from love.

A healer named Robin shared the following experience:

"A master guide was traveling with me through a deep forest. The forest appeared to be a rain forest, lush and pristine. We were

climbing up through the most beautiful area as he showed me the intricacies and delicately formed plants that made up the region. I was enjoying this immensely, but questioned what this had to do with healing. I wanted to see the 'big picture.'

He said gently, 'Turn around.' Turning around, I found myself looking at the universe just as it had appeared in the Hubble telescope pictures I had seen. The swirls of colors, vast spaces and clear stars and planets took my breath away. I was IN the picture. It was such an incredible experience. I asked, 'Help me understand.'

He told me that it was all the same, the intricacies of the rain forest and the vastness of the universe; it is all the same, just different energies, different manifestations. That was what he was trying to explain to me. We are all made up of energies that have to be aligned to be in balance, just as the rain forest has to stay in balance or be destroyed."

There is a direction to life and a purpose. The journey of healing requires that we find spiritual direction.

To heal, we do not have to start at the base, the root chakra, and work our way up. The shortest and most direct path to healing is through the sixth chakra and crown. A daily spiritual practice opens these centers to God's light and sound, which in turn allows us to have a broader viewpoint in all areas of our lives, including our health.

God is continually communicating Its intention, love, and vision for our lives. Soul is continually communicating its reason for being. A daily spiritual exercise, or contemplation, clears the channel between the human consciousness and soul so that we can hear the spiritual voice.

There are two parts to God's voice, the Holy Spirit—the creative out-breath, and the in-breath, which draws all of life back to It. Our human experience models the divine expression. Our in-breath is our time of contemplation and reflection in which we receive divine love and inspiration; our out-breath is the life we create and the service and love we return to life. We don't stop at hearing the music of God; we must give back the song through the lives that we live and the love that we are.

This is the secret to co-creating health and a life that we love.